FIRST EDITIC

It is not the purpose of this book to diagnose or treat any disease. Where there is concern about health matters, or when symptoms persist, professional advice from a health practitioner should be sought.

ISBN 0 9530948 0 4

Published by NUHELTH BOOKS
Church Street, Stroud, Gloucestershire GL5 1JL, England

Designed, Typeset and Printed by
Omega Print & Design Ltd., Cheshire.

Printed in England

C O N T E N T S

Dr. Hugo Brandenberger

DEDICATION

When I first had the idea of writing a book on organic juices it was my intention to cover the whole variety of fruits and vegetables available for juicing, based on my accumulated knowledge and experience.

As I progressed with the task it become obvious that too few of the fruits and vegetables were available in sufficient or commercial quantities. So whilst I plead that only organic fruit and vegetable juices should be used for therapeutic purposes, there seems little point in repeating what many other juice books have already said, if the juices in that form are not readily available. Therefore this book covers a range of vegetable juices which are always available in Britain and other countries and have, over the last thirty or more years, proved their worth, in my experience.

We live in an age of convenience. When time is of the essence it is usually impractical and often climatically unfavourable to plant organic produce, nurture it to maturity, pick it and take it indoors to extract the juice electronically. For whilst fresh may be best, it is not always possible within the constraints of today's pace of life.

For this reason I wish to dedicate this book to four people who have, by their example, influenced the lives of many, many thousands of people with their contribution to the production of truly live organic juices in a form that is readily available, easy to use and completely reliable.

They are, first, Dr Hugo Brandenberger, who had the foresight, knowledge and experience to see the potential of the Tagerwilen land and to progress Biotta to the primary organic fruit and vegetable juice producing company in Switzerland, maybe in the world, and to do this without compromising standards or exploiting his work force. A man of deeply sincere simple religious conviction, which is the infrastructure of his creation.

Second, for Christian Brandenberger, his son, who admirably

chose to follow his father's footsteps; and from a menial start, has progressed through the company to the top position today. That he has also chosen to adopt those same ethical philosophies within the business in this day and age is a credit to him and his paternal mentor.

What do I say about Willi Egli? A delightful man with a witty and vibrant personality - a man at one with the soil and its produce - dedicated, loyal, friendly, determined, strong, talented with both language and music, but above all a man with an innate understanding of nature. Few people would have time every morning to visit each plant in their garden, to observe and discuss with it its progress. The plants are to him like children - to be nurtured, cared for and understood. As my host and guide on a visit to the Biotta production centre he was impressive. There cannot be another like Willi Egli in all the world and I wish him well in his retirement.

Last, but by no means least, the late Rudolf Breuss. A humble man of extraordinary talent - a born healer. Motivated to discover a simple and effective natural treatment for so many cancers and other serious conditions as a result of witnessing the trauma so often experienced by people undergoing radiation, chemotherapy and surgery. Few electrical engineers would deign to question the work of eminent surgeons and medical consultants whose specialist subject is oncology, and say 'there must be a natural alternative to what they are doing'! He did just that and found it; had the courage to practise it for thirty years; then, on retirement, put down his system in detail for anyone to follow in his now well known book which has sold over 850,000 copies (the whole of Chapter 9 is devoted to Rudolf Breuss).

He was a painstaking herbalist with great understanding of the therapeutic use of herb teas. A man whose diagnostic ability of looking into the iris of the eye was such that he could pinpoint disease with great accuracy throughout the body.
My time with him was special and will always be remembered. For me, he was one of those rare beings whom it is a real privilege to have known.

INTRODUCTION

It is fifty years since I first saw the value of Nature Cure working. Like many converts to this healing system it was the result of family illness.

As a child brought up in a working class environment in Birmingham we had lived through the war, survived the blitz and some of the 'new' medicine - the sulphonamides and antibiotics - of the 1940's.

The diet had been and was still restricted by rationing. There was little fruit about and not much choice of vegetables either.

So my school years were sickly ones as I seemed to catch everything that happened to be around the Midlands - all the childhood diseases and more! I have memories of days in a cold bedroom upstairs - because if you were ill you went to bed - when you were up and about you went to school. I do not recall being 'up' at home unless it was a holiday.

In those days the doctor called - it was a rare occasion to visit the surgery. Perhaps my parents were over cautious - or getting their money's worth, because one paid for medical treatment. And the doctor offered the service. The more times he was called out the more he earned. I must have been a very good customer in commercial terms. "Your child suffers from acidosis" was the ultimate diagnosis. And that spelled years on a fat free diet - because it was the belief in those days that fat - butter, cheese, milk, oils, fat meat and all foods containing these - was the culprit! I suppose it was something that the doctor even considered the problem might be dietetic! Orthodox medicine did not consider illness, particularly chronic, to be caused by dietetic indisposition in the post war years. However, I was not to know the value of choosing one's food more carefully until many years later.

At that time it was simply a chore and there was little enjoyment in eating - so I didn't. Or to be more precise I was finicky. Particularly as I did not much enjoy the 'right foods' anyway. Meat and potatoes were the staple diet - the former because protein was 'good for you' and potatoes 'filled you up'.

In the health stakes my mother did not enjoy good odds either. Not surprising really - the usual devitalised diet of the day - difficult pregnancy and horrific birth. I nearly died and so did my mother. - That must have been traumatic. I'm glad I don't remember. Strangely she went through this again with the birth of my brother, but not so badly. However, it was against good advice and a price was paid.

That paints a picture of childhood. I'm sure it wasn't really all like that. It just seems like it when reviewing my early years from a health angle.

However, my health had nothing to do with my conversion. It was my mother's which opened my eyes to a whole new way of living. For she was then on the large side - 13 stone to be precise and about 5 feet tall. She had great difficulty coping with the daily housewifely and motherly business. As the crisis point loomed it became impossible for her to even climb the stairs without having to sit and rest half way! Then it happened. I arrived home from school to be told by my anxious father that Mum was in hospital.

I never did find out what happened but it must have been a collapse of some sort or another for she was there for weeks as she was rested and tested.

Then one day she was home again - but very ill. I was later to find out she had come home to die. The diagnosis was degeneration of the liver for which there was no known orthodox cure. The prognosis was a maximum of two years to live, but probably less. What must my father have felt at the time? His wife in her thirties and two young children to nurture.

Despite my father's very orthodox mind, on this occasion he searched to find an alternative method of treatment which would reverse the doctors conclusion.

By the by, one should always look for the positive reasons in any traumatic event. There is always a lesson to be learned as life inexorably drives one forward. In retrospect this must have been my father's lesson to move his thinking from the effortless attitude which so many people have towards orthodox medicine - that inbuilt faith in the doctor's ability to restore the health of the individual. Here he was presented with a *fait accompli* which so many people endure when the doctor says, 'There is nothing more we can do'.

Looking back my father must have been far less fixed in attitude of mind, because he did not accept that doctor's word as final. He chose to look to other avenues for help. And it is this which is perhaps the most important message to be carried through the pages of this book.

We are mortal and we are all fallible. It is, therefore, every sick person's right to seek help from any of the healing faculties or systems. No one system has the authority to pronounce on a person's life expectancy. It may be that orthodox medicine will say,'There is nothing more we can do'. But it does not mean that other methods of healing should not be investigated and indeed tried.

For it is a fact that untold numbers of people have been saved by alternative medicine - be it any system from fasting and dietetics to the laying on of hands. I have seen it personally in my own family on more than one occasion and I have witnessed it in many other families too. And so it was that my father found the Nut & Carrot Man of Sutton Coldfield as he was affectionately known by the kindly cynics, and as AJ by the devoted.
To cut a long story short my mother entered a period of dietetic adjustment which was to last long past the two year life expectancy medical pronouncement. As we saw the body weight diminish by more than half to a mere six stone (91 pounds or 41.33 kilos).

Gradually by a process of elimination, together with a cleansing and nourishing diet, the body was rebuilt, but on a sounder base. And with this foundation she was to live another forty years, in excellent health. before passing on some six hours after a stroke, caused by a previously damaged sub-arachnoid artery, the result of a car accident in her early twenties.

Clearly, this experience, along with the subtle changes made to my diet, and its rewards, influenced my way of life. And some years later I was privileged to be taught the practice of nature cure by this same man Mr A J Badham - the practice of using food, liquids, herbs of the field, sun, air, water and exercise as the means of promoting a healthy and vigorous lifestyle.

My own 'acidosis' succumbed to a properly balanced diet including a preponderance of fruit and vegetables and their juices.

A brief mono diet of grapefruit juice quelled my wife's serious pregnancy sickness - why didn't I think of it earlier?!

Vegetable juices administered over thirty years ago to my second son were the nurturing replacement of milk in any form, including breast, which he could not seem to tolerate.
Then there was the influence of such early Nature Cure writers as Dr Kirschner, John Lust and Norman Walker and their experiences with fruit and vegetable juices. However, my most touching experiences were my meetings and conversations with the eminent Austrian practitioner Rudolf Breuss and some of his ex-patients. His book; *Cancer/Leukaemia and Other Seemingly Incurable Diseases* led me to his home where, at the grand old age of eighty two he told me all about his use of vegetable juices as part of a natural treatment of certain cancers. To this I have given a whole chapter in this book since it is a marvellous and incredibly simple system which has enjoyed much success both during his practice, before he retired some years ago, and in the homes of vast numbers of persons all over the world. In these days of strong and powerful drugs, the almost indiscriminate use of radiation therapy, the many and various organ transplants and radical surgery, it is my hope and wish that this book will offer you an opportunity, when ready, to explore the more simplistic and natural methods of growing organically, living in harmony with nature and using her fruits of the earth for nourishment and health.

CHAPTER ONE

THE GROWTH OF ORGANICS IN BRITAIN

As mentioned through this book, the value of organically grown food cannot be over-estimated and it is interesting that in England and many other countries there is today a greater drive towards organic agriculture.

It has always been there, but carried out only by a few dedicated farmers and growers.

However, the ever increasing public concern about the pollution of the atmosphere, coupled with the use of chemical fertilisers and pesticides, has led those discerning campaigners to look to farmers in the hope of persuading them to reform their method of intensive farming and start producing by the long established organic method. The residues of chemical treatment of crops in food offered to the consumer is worrying and not before time. For one has seen on occasion the results of an accumulation of these chemicals in the body tissues. DDT is a prime example.

The whole problem of chemical or intensive farming has now spread to contaminate the water supplies in various areas of the country. Nitrate pollution is a disturbing matter as consumption can be carcinogenic to humans and animals alike.

The nitrates find their way from the land into the rivers and streams. Even the water table well beneath the surface is becoming contaminated.

Man has a lot to answer for in his drive for greater crop cultivation at any cost. When one considers that much of this bounty is over production to be stored, often for a long time, it seems madness. That these stored products require further treatment by chemicals to preserve them only makes the whole business bizarre. Yet eminent politicians, well educated businessmen and those close to the land insist it is necessary to feed the people. And in many parts of the world millions are starving! Such is the way when common sense is overtaken by economics.

I have always been wary of the EEC, ever since I discovered that the second E stood for 'Economic'. As time seems to prove, the European Economic Community (now the EU-European Union) has so far been anything but economic. The member states have poured more and more money into it year after year in the futile hope that the rewards will come. When will they learn that the law of supply and demand is axiomatic? Perhaps this new arousal of the public will stimulate more farmers to opt for meeting the demands of an ever more watchful public and they will turn their acres over to the organic system. A system which by dictionary definition describes organic when applied to food as 'produced without artificial fertilisers or pesticides'. It is, of course, much more than that. Prohibiting the use of soluble chemical salts and all agro-chemicals must be replaced by a method of growing which was the norm prior to the advent of 'pharmaceutical' farming. That includes crop rotation, the use of animal and vegetable manures and, where necessary, the protection of crops with natural products.

Some growers go further and practise biological pest control. This means introducing the predators of those insects which cause damage to crops. Others will grow one product with another which affords protection to the main crop for example, a line of onions alongside a line of green beans because the pests which attack the beans do not like the onions.

In the UK it is estimated there are about 500 people farming organically over an area of 14,000 acres. This represents barely one per cent of the farming population. But it is growing and all the signs are that it will grow at a faster pace between now and the end of this century. These figures do not take account of the many market gardeners and smallholdings which use the organic method. And these are responsible for the production of most of the home grown fruit and vegetables. Organic cereals are the principle crops of the farmer.

More than 60% of organic food consumed in the UK has to be imported from lands all over the world. But mostly from the more organically advanced countries in Europe and the American continent. However, the percentage of fruit imported is considerably higher than the overall 60%, mainly because few UK fruit farmers have resisted the temptation to use chemicals, and our climate does not encourage the production of many of the fruits demanded by the consumer. Neither does the cost of the European legislation imposed by Parliament on organic growers with small orchards, perhaps a few fruit trees, encourage production. In fact many have given up because their fruit cannot be described as organic without lots of paperwork and the payment of an exorbitant fee out of all proportion to the crop yield. And the nation loses more home production of all sorts of varieties in favour of mass produced entities, mostly from abroad!

TAGERWILEN - AN ORGANIC OASIS

Because of the limited fruit and vegetable production in Britain, particularly on a large scale, I sought advice and help from the Swiss, who have long been recognised as the pioneers of organic farming in Europe, thanks to the work of two great men, Dr Hans Muller and Dr Rudolf Steiner.

I was recommended to visit Biotta AG situated in the small village of Tagerwilen near Kreutzlingen, lying in that rich and fertile portion of land bordered by the mountains and the northern part of the River Rhine. The climatic conditions due to neighbouring Lakes Konstanze and Unter, together with an alluvial land, makes this a perfect spot for vegetable production, and this was recognised a very long time ago.

I had known of the Biotta company since their products were available throughout the world and have been sold in health food stores in the UK for thirty years or more. But their name had even greater meaning for me as the makers of the Breuss Vegetable Juice, a special formula or organically grown juices produced for the famous Austrian natural healer Rudolf Breuss. This requires a chapter all of its own later in the book. I approached the company and asked if I could see their system of agriculture through to the final production of the juices.

In typical Swiss fashion I was warmly welcomed and allowed access to anything and everything available. My host, Herr Willi Egli was their Food Technologist at the time and his knowledge and understanding of the finer points of organic production is probably unsurpassed today and almost certainly in his lifetime. Since he could speak English well there was no communication problem and I looked forward to a detailed investigation into the world of organic fruit and vegetable production.

In order to understand the dedication Willi Egli has to both the principles and practice of growing organic food and his total loyalty to the company Biotta, I must say a little about the man.

Describing his title as Food Technologist gives a false indication of a boffin type individual - scientific and serious. Willi Egli is short, strong, stocky and was in his sixties at the time. He has a powerful voice, doubtless a result of his many 'vocations' as a captain and disciplinarian in the Swiss Army. He has a smile and a laugh and charm likely to capture the most critical of persons. He is a one-off who has an intuitive understanding of man and nature. A man who enjoys life and meets and makes the most of each day as it comes. He is close to the soil as one would expect and has a spiritual reverence for life which is there throughout each day. And in this he is quite serious. Like many disciplined servicemen he is a man of strict routine. He does not leave his house each morning without first walking round his garden to visit the plants and herbs. He alights the train he takes to work one stop before Tagerwilen so he can 'march' the last miles - for the exercise. He insists on a silent minute each day to remember God and nature. A visit to the village church at lunchtime to play the organ. And *"Ve must sing Meester Hill"* he implored me *"it is important for the development of ze 'eart and lungs.* And each day one must drink vegetable juice and eat some herbs".

Yes, this man is unique, I thought, as I found myself running to keep up with him. *"Ve vill start now"* he announced. And with a hefty slap on the back which removed the last vestige of air remaining in an already overworked pair of lungs we were on our way - the beginning of three days into the depths and vagaries of the Biotta production cycle from seed to juice.

I learned the company was founded in 1931 as a market garden growing vegetables. Its conversion to organic cultivation took place in 1951. And there was a period of six years before the first organic vegetables were introduced in 1957.
At least a five year period was considered to be the conversion time before soil was sufficiently cleared of chemical residues in order to call the product grown in it 'organic'.

As I looked over the one hundred and twenty thousand square

metres of land I could not but think how many other smallholders here and elsewhere could have developed in much the same way as have Biotta. For they, like most pioneers, proceeded from small beginnings.

"There are thirty thousand square metres of glass houses" Herr Egli volunteered.

It was massive. A single glasshouse appeared enormous as one entered.

"And twenty thousand square metres are heated" he added.

Strange though it may be, I was first and foremost interested in the compost heap, because I have always believed that it is this which puts life into the soil.

So our first call was to a large area, about as long as a football pitch and half as wide, which was devoted to lines of compost. And I saw them adding at one end and taking away at the other. The latter being the consistency of a rich brown soil, whilst the former was still 'green'.

This rich compost is made up of ground waste and is turned once a month. 'Green manure' as Biotta describe it, which comprises clover, vetch and oats, is harrowed straight into the soil as part of the rotation system. Animal manure is also added to the soil. Particular care is taken with organic cultivation to ensure that the billions of living organisms and creatures contained in just a single handful of soil are able to function without disturbance. These living organisms and creatures are absolutely necessary for preparing and providing nutrients for the plants.

The nutrients permeate through the soil into the roots of the plant and subsequently into animals and human beings. Finally, whenever possible, to be returned to the soil in the form of manure.

It is this wonderful cycle of living substance which Biotta tap into, always trying to avoid anything which may destroy it.

The Biotta Organic Farm and Juice Production Plant in Tagerwilen, close to Lake Konstanz in Switzerland

Willi Egli talks enthusiastically about the organic production of Biotta juices to a group of health store owners from the U.K.

As I thought about this I was reminded of Dr Max Bircher's principles about the importance of eating raw fruits and vegetables. For here it is borne out and practised. His tenets offered nearly 70 years ago maintained that the consumption of live raw food will cure up to 80% of all disease.

Let us go into the difference between conventional chemical growing and organic at this crucial point. Because if nothing else, I believe anyone switching from eating conventionally grown food to that grown by this simplistic and wholly natural organic way will derive great benefits.

The purely chemical fertilization as used for the last forty years or so in agriculture might be compared with food in tablet form. Such a method can certainly provide the desired quantity, but it cannot produce quality. The application of highly growth boosting artificial fertilisers creates a reduction in the plants' resistance to disease and parasites. This sets off a chain reaction of continuously intensifying the demand for chemical pesticides and other agents for controlling plant disease.

This emphasises in the plant world the basic doctrine of the practice of Nature Cure or Naturopathic Medicine as applied to human beings. It is that - there is but one disease, lowered vitality. Which means that in a healthy body germs, viruses and the like, will not and cannot develop. It is the state of the host which creates the 'soil' upon which these foreign and unwelcome guests can develop or not. Anything which lowers the vitality should be avoided for one who wishes to enjoy good health. It is this almost mystical vitality or life force which allows us to function efficiently. Research work conducted at the Aaran and Basle cantonal hospitals revealed that breast milk in Switzerland contained up to forty times more pesticides than internationally permissible in normal cows milk! The effect of this on future generations fills one with a sense of foreboding unless there is action to reverse this quickly. The lay observer might wonder if this one factor is a contribution to the ever increasing incidence of breast cancer and allergies.

Organic cultivation offers a true alternative to the chemical and environmentally crude and burdensome method. It affords top priority to the maintenance and care of the soil bacteria. This is because a good overall soil quality is a vital prerequisite for healthy and highly resistant plants at Biotta, artificial fertilisers and poisonous sprays are never used.

In Switzerland two schools of organic agriculture have emerged; the biological-dynamic method as developed along the lines of the teachings laid down by Dr Rudolf Steiner. The other being the organic-biological cultivation method developed by Dr Hans Muller who, over many years has converted hundreds of farming establishments to his system. It is this system which is used at Biotta. After a life of extraordinary achievement Dr Muller died at the grand age of 97. There are now some five hundred farms belonging to the cooperative society he founded and known as the 'Bio-gemuse Genossenschaft Galmiz'. It is some of these farms which supplement the vegetables grown by Biotta. They are, in fact, major suppliers.

The controls applied to the farms are very sound in that the products are regularly tested to ensure there are no chemical residues. And since each farmer has a considerable sum of money lodged with the organisation, he would actually lose that should he be found not to be producing organically.

Dr Muller's organic-biological system insists on:

● Ground waste to compost which must be turned once a month.

● Mount Gotthard minerals being fed to the soil since this activates and disinfects quicker, thus keeping the vegetables healthy. This mineral supplement comprises Calcium, Magnesium and Silica.

● A seven year rotation of vegetables with three years left to nature to allow the ground to regenerate.

● Definitely no mono-culture and each field having three crops. For instance Celeriac, Carrots and Cabbage.

Clearly this method works tremendously well, as all the crops I saw looked very healthy. And as anyone knows who has lived in Switzerland, the fresh Biotta salad vegetables sold in most food outlets are second to none in their quality.

During the period between 1981 and 1983 a laboratory in Basle examined 646 samples of conventially grown fruit and vegetables of which 37% showed measurable residues of pesticides. Yet over the same period 118 samples taken from organically grown produce did not reveal any pesticides at all.

However, this is not the only difference between the two types. There is what Biotta describe as an 'inner quality' which, with advanced modern scientific methods and detailed trials and tests, it is now possible to prove. Later in this book, when I talk about my experiences with Rudolf Breuss, I will illustrate my own proof of efficacy - unconventional though it may be.

Some years ago Dr E Aehnelt and Professor J Hahn of the Hanover University in Germany had proved that sperm from animals fed with conventionally grown fodder lose their fertility after four days almost completely, whilst it is fully alive for six days in animals fed with organically grown fodder. In simple terms, these animals were no longer able to pass the seed of life after eating chemically treated food.

As we walked round Willi Egli was so eager to give me information - the enthusiasm was contagious. I found myself actually coming to terms with the soil and the whole system of plant growth. In fact it was an extraordinary experience to contemplate the infinite workings of nature - here it was being explained to me very simply by a person who was finally attuned to the whole process of the cycle. From the soil and its bacteria or living organism to the final plant was an absorbing and fascinating experience - made possible only be someone who truly understands.

It is a different world from commercial and conventional farming and growing which has really become an instrument of the laboratory - if you have this disease you hit it with this chemical and for that disease you hit it with another! The preventative side is met with chemical fertilisers to 'improve' an already impoverished soil and pesticides to ward away the myriad of insects which form on any plant without the 'inner quality' or bounding vitality.

Sounds just like orthodox medical practice. It's no wonder there is a continuing and growing demand for more hospitals and doctors. Like the farming laboratories they have become caught in a descending spiral of administering chemical medicine which ensures the plant (land) or patient gives up the ghost!

It is a fact that large corporate bodies and pharmaceutical houses of great reputation cannot survive on the proceeds of a compost heap or good organic husbandry.

"The ground should always have green cover" Willi Egli told me. "A handful of organic soil contains more bacteria than there are people in the whole world" he confided. "They must be protected" he went on, "so always cover the soil against too hot a summer or too cold a winter".

"And never ever change the ground. Turn no more than 12 centimetres. The bacteria live in 30 centimetres. Then you will get a healthy product" he concluded. When I asked later how they were sure the farmers who grew the vegetables for them obeyed the rules he told me "We analyse the soil in every field of every farmer once a year".

We moved on through one glasshouse to another - a living carpet of chlorophyll in the form of cress - another full of thousands of tomato seedlings - a third surprisingly packed with show winning chrysanthemums. It was all part of the rotation system. Then there was row upon row of lettuce. "We used to plant all these by hand which was very labour intensive" Herr Egli commented, "but now we do it by machine and that allows us to sell them at a competitive price to conventially-grown ones".

There were, of course, outdoor varieties too. 120,000 in just one field, of which 12,000 will be picked in a single day.

When I questioned the fact that there were weeds growing with them I was told weeding only occurs when they are likely to interfere with the growth of the lettuce. Once the field is clear all the weeds are worked into the ground providing 'green manure'.

As a matter of interest, Biotta have a distribution system using their own vehicles which go to the wholesaler, and during the night, to the retailer, so the customer gets the Biotta vegetables in an absolutely fresh condition, almost as though they had picked them from their own garden. Twenty four hours from harvesting to the customer!

It was similar too with cauliflowers where one can distinguish the difference between those where chemical fertilisers have been used. The latter have a rather unpleasant smell.

We came to the glasshouse containing cucumbers. It is not easy to take in the fact that Biotta pick no fewer than half a million organically grown cucumbers every year.

However, cucumbers can be subject to pest and disease, not least the dreaded red spider.

"This is an instance where we utilise biological control of pests" my host and guide informed me. "We have introduced the South American Rubber Mite and that deals with the Red Spider. This really is a great help to us".

I noticed too that the soil in the cucumber house was covered with weeds, which I discovered were there to protect the soil life and to maintain soil humidity. It also yields to the soil fresh supplies of organic substances.

Biotta pick 250 tonnes of tomatoes from row after row of a particular fleshy variety ideally suited for salads, and half a million cucumbers.

Between these rows is a groundcover of clover which acts not only as 'green manure' but it also protects the soil and enriches it with nitrogen.

I thought of all the water that was required to keep all these plants in good condition. I might have known. It comes from the passing river Rhine by way of a special pump system. It goes into tanks where it is injected with a special bacterial culture. They would use a million litres of water on a hot day.

Both on the land and in the glasshouses Biotta offer a magnificent example of how it is possible to produce a whole range of produce by organic methods on a massive scale.

We were now on our way to the factory where the vegetables are prepared and turned into juice.

Christian Brandenberger discusses the latest crop of ripe peppers with one of his dedicated team.

One of the giant juice extractors pressing thousands of gallons of fresh, pure carrot juice which runs down to the enormous vats in the basement below. It is whilst in these vats, prior to bottling, that the special lactic acid process takes place - preserving the juice naturally without spoiling the taste.

CHAPTER THREE

JUICE PRODUCTION AT TAGERWILEN

The first thing I came across was not juice, but tonnes and tonnes of cabbages, all organically produced.

"We make the best Sauerkraut in Switzerland" Herr Egli stated, full of extrovert enthusiasm. It was as if we had discovered a whole new world in gourmet eating. "You must try some" he declared. So I did and it was delicious.

The cabbage goes through a strict process from the time the outside green leaves are removed during picking to leave lovely white cabbage hearts. As they arrive at the factory the stalks are bored out and the cabbage sliced.

These slices then go into enormous silos containing thirty tonnes. First a layer of cabbage, followed by a layer of herbs and spices, then another layer of cabbage and so on until it is full. The silo is closed and the lactic fermentation begins which transforms the sliced cabbage into their now famous Sauerkraut.

This special process was developed by Walter Kogler of Stein am Rhein but originally from Bohemia, as a perfect method for the production of Sauerkraut. He actually presented his recipe to Biotta to ensure its continuity. It takes about five weeks before the final fermentation takes place. At which point it is packed into bags ready to be sold. Biotta do not use any heat treatment or any type of preservative and I was reliably informed during my visit that it was the only one on the market which keeps for months without pasteurisation.

This process is, of course, necessary in order to produce Sauerkraut juice, an important part of the Biotta healing juices. But which, unfortunately, is not yet available in Britain.

Many farmers around and beyond Tagerwilen are contracted to

grow root vegetables which are used to produce the juices. All these farmers abide by the standards laid down by Dr Hans Muller for producing organic crops. And they belong to the Bio-Vegetable Production Association.

There are hundreds of these farmers who follow the method which is very strictly controlled. One day perhaps we shall have a similar operation in the U.K and perhaps maybe in all countries of the world, as people realise the futility of continuously using chemicals on the land, with its consequent deterioration of the soil, let alone the crop's subsequent effect on the consumer!

During the busy months from August to the Spring as much as two thousand tonnes of organically produced beetroot, carrots, celeriacs and potatoes are delivered in from the surrounding farms every day. This is an enormous quantity by any standards. That it is all organic is truly impressive.

Once the vegetables have been inspected and checked for quality and purity in terms of organic standards they are prepared for juicing. Biotta have a particular method of testing for organic, as opposed to non organic crops, which is known as the Bio-Test and it will be described when we explore the value to health of the use of fruit and vegetable juices in the diet.

The vegetables are washed and thoroughly cleaned on a long wash belt which is run on the contra-current principle. This has the effect of forcing dirt off the roots until they emerge beautifully clean - clean enough to eat without any further preparation. The water is absolutely pure, nothing is added, no detergents of any kind.
It has always concerned me that many systems of cleaning vegetables in the U.K and on the Continent involve the use of chemicals and one wonders how much is left on and in the vegetable after it has been subjected to these artificial cleaning methods.

It was a delight to see that in each process from growing to the finished product the company has thought of everything to guarantee the product is presented as a purely unadulterated food.

Once the vegetables have gone through the washing process they are taken by conveyor into larger presses for the juice to be extracted. To give some impression of the size and capacity of these machines is difficult with words, but when one understands that there is a pressure of nearly a quarter of a million kilogrammes bearing down on the vegetables in order to extract the juice, it paints a picture. For they are not dealing with a soft pulped fruit where there is plenty of moisture to extract, but rather solid, hard and fibrous roots which, at a glance, would deem as being devoid of any liquid.

That is until one sees the juice flow from these presses. Gallons and gallons of pure juice runs down to enormous vats in the basement of the building. Here it has added to it a special lactic acid process which improves the quality of the juice and its preservation. This use of a lactic acid formulation is a very important process because it succeeds in preserving the juice without spoiling the taste. And it is very much a secret process since I am assured nobody has yet perfected such a method of bottling natural juices as Biotta have without losing or altering the original flavour.

Anyone who has compared the juice from a fresh orange with that purporting to be natural from a can, tetrapak, carton or bottle will confirm this. Except, one has to say, when tasting Biotta. But there is more to say on the subject.

Following the addition of the special lactic acid to the fresh juice, it is then passed through to stainless steel storage tanks, each of which has a capacity of twenty thousand litres.

The dry fibrous waste from the juice process, which represents 50% of the original root, is used as fodder for the animals, which is converted into manure to feed the land.

The care that is taken is indicated by the number of checks made by Biotta's own laboratory during the whole process. Not only do they go to the farms and check the soil in the farmers' fields and the crop yield as it arrives at the juice factory, but they examine the juice before and after the lactic acidification to ensure its authenticity and quality.

Much of what I have been saying concerning factory systems may appear obvious to the informed reader. But it is necessary to understand that I am not simply observing a system, but actually applying a critical eye in order to evaluate methods in light of what they say they do and what does happen in fact. Not all advertising blurb is a messenger of the truth!

I wanted to know exactly what occurs which was why I went to see for myself.

After more than thirty five years in the health food movement my eyes have been opened more than once by a bit of amateur detection and the right questions at the wrong time! And I do not believe the public, and not least a public seeking health and healthy alternatives to mass produced junk food, should be duped into accepting something which is not what it is alleged to be. Therefore I will only write about that which I have seen and which pleases my sense of propriety.

Was there not a chink in the Biotta armour? An Achilles heel which might lead me to a misdemeanour, however minor? If there was I never found it - despite days of wandering around the whole business.
Even their bottles are always pure recycled glass and disposable. "Many people have suggested that we should use returnable bottles" I was told. "But once you do this they have to be cleaned with strong chemicals which are harmful to the environment".

Then I learned of the collection of used glass which occurs throughout Switzerland, where two thirds of the glass is recycled in the glass works. This really is so obvious and simple and it is good to see it happening in Britain too these days. The Biotta glass is always dark tinted so there is no oxidation. Thus their pure vegetable juices do not lose their nutritional value as do those open to the light through clear glass.

An electronically controlled filling plant puts through as many as fifteen thousand bottles an hour or something like one hundred thousand bottles a day. And each bottle is sterilised with hot water before it is finally filled.

It is this careful process coupled with the lactic acid process which gives the taste of freshly pressed juice.

From the time the vegetables are placed in the washing troughs, to the point where the filled bottles are stored in boxes on pallets in a massive warehouse, there is no human contact. It all happens using ultra modern hygienic machinery, thus avoiding any possible risk of contamination.

By its very nature vegetable pressing is a seasonal business. Obviously the juice is best pressed from vegetables just hours after they have been picked. And this is what Biotta do. So their warehouses have capacity for storing no less than four million bottles. And like so many Swiss products they are exported widely.

For more than thirty years it has been on sale in Britain and I know it is available in most continental countries. But they now send it to America and Canada to meet the ever increasing demand for quality organically grown food.

From Switzerland one now travels to Israel to a Kibbutz where oranges and grapefruits are grown strictly in accordance with Biotta biological principles, which they have been supervising for the past twenty years. It produces thousands of tonnes of fruit annually.

Biological pest control with the use of insects is highly developed in Israel. A virus is used to control the Shield Louse and the Mediterranean Fly is kept in check by the daily production of flies which are made sterile by X-ray treatment. These flies are released to mate without reproducing.

Specially constructed machines have been designed to press the fruit, which produces a juice free from pip, pith or skin.

The Biotta organically grown Orange Juice and Grapefruit Juice is pure juice exactly as it comes from the fruit. It has not been subjected to a drying process to be economically shipped and, once landed, to be reconstituted - having water added to it.

It seems to me grossly unfair that packers of many of the well known brands of various juices are allowed to use the words 'pure' and 'natural' on bottles, tins and tetrapaks when the product is certainly not natural by any stretch of the imagination. How can it possibly be when the very liquid which was in the fruit at the time it was picked has been systematically removed by a process designed to leave a dry mass?

This powder then has water added to it which by British standards can hardly be described as pure. According to recent reports, water in the U.K does not even meet current EU standards and we have always been warned in this country never to drink water from the tap on the continent! Such is the deterioration of British water supplies, if not in all areas of the country, then in parts.
It is the misuse of the word 'natural' by unscrupulous advertising people that will either force the powers that be to ban or severely control its use on packaging and advertising in the future, or the public will cease to recognise it as an honest descriptive word and it will lose its value.

At the time of writing the country is going through a stage where practically everything in a packet is described as natural simply because there is no accurate legislation to control its use.

So let us not be confused by words which are beginning to lose their true meaning. And in this regard I notice Biotta are describing their citrus juices as being freshly squeezed. This does at least convey the message that the juice is just as it comes from the fruit. And that can be proven by the taste. Which is more than can be said for the reconstituted varieties. In Israel soil samples are taken by the Ministry of Agriculture and each consignment of fruit receives an official analysis report confirming that the fruits are pure and free from chemical residue.

Meanwhile, in the South Tyrol of Italy, organic land yields more fruit. This time it is by the cultivation of succulent grapes and blackcurrants. These are monitored by a local biologist who performs checks on the soil and ensures the produce is free from any form of artificial chemical. A second control is carried out by the official government control organisation for biological production (AIAP).

Organically grown vegetables - from seedlings.

CHAPTER FOUR

A CHEMICAL DILEMMA

In earlier chapters we have seen that the use of artificial fertilisers developed from the fact that plants need nitrogen, phosphorous, potassium and chalk. Where these are given in their inorganic form this simply equates to the taking of mineral supplements by humans - it supplies quantity but not necessarily quality.

There are two questions - is it absorbed by the body of plant or human and put to good use? And if it is, does it in itself upset what is a very fine nutritional balance?

I do not profess to be an expert in the field of isolated vitamin and mineral supplementation, but he has a functioning intuition which says that these nutrients work together to create a whole and this includes all sorts of trace elements and enzymes acting in harmony. The moment one alters this harmony from without by taking in harmful substances, be it carbon monoxide from vehicle exhausts, for instance, or radioactive emissions from nuclear power stations, or perhaps the more esoteric rays from the national grid which carries electricity around the country - there is a chain of events which takes place to which I am not yet certain man has the answer.

This is amply illustrated by the use of artificial fertilisers which then create a need for chemical pesticides, herbicides, fungicides et al. In other words, the balance of nature has been disturbed and an insidious series of events occur which effectively pollutes the land, the rivers and the consumer.

In human terms the result of using chemical fertilisers creates a need for chemical pesticides which is often retained by the plant, thus consumed by man, which affects the health of the individual. The proof that this chemical warfare on the plant kingdom is detrimental to the body is in its ability to store these harmful ingested chemicals in the fat tissue from whence they will do the least harm. Unless of course you are a lactating female and this residue will be passed through to the infant by way of breast milk.

I remember during my early days in Nature Cure practice we were instructed to no longer carry out the longer fasts on patients which our pioneer forbears had used so successfully in years past. The reason for this was the overuse of DDT by farmers treating their crops. It was so rife among foodstuffs few human bodies were without a fair quantity accumulating in the body fat.

Once a fast had undergone the initial few days of cleansing, the body controls went to work on the excess fat tissue. This had the effect of releasing into the bloodstream significant quantities of DDT which poisoned the patient. Although this vicious pesticide was voluntarily withdrawn years ago, I suspect there are many others which have taken its place.

As to water fasting - yes of course it is still a valuable cleansing method, but a few days at a time, short and more often is the order of the day. However, it does take longer to purify the system, but at least it is safer. Fasting on vegetable juices is much safer over a long period.

It is not as though there was not an alternative to chemical farming. Growing organically has been around for eons. It is simply that man does seem to want things easier and quicker. And generally he seems to have more respect for the pharmaceutical technician than for nature.

CHAPTER FIVE

MEN OF VISION

The nature based agricultural system of organic biological law as devised by Dr Hans Muller gave Biotta all it needed to produce top quality food.

Dr Hans Peter Rusch used his scientific knowledge to provide what is now known as the Rusch Test for soil and is used by Biotta to test whether a particular field has achieved an organic standard. This is done basically by subjecting the soil to a microscopical bacteria test.

In Dr Rusch's words - "It is the aim of organic, biological farming to be responsible for the health of mankind through the production of living nourishment. The biologically healthy earth is composed of a microflora of billions of living things per cubic centimetre, which have the task of providing nutrition to the plants, giving man and animals food of full nutritional value".

It was the economic method which was introduced and encouraged by Dr Muller. The plants were nourished with a qualitative as well as quantitative microflora without the use of poisonous insecticides and artificial fertilisers.

The dedication of these men was complemented by a third man of letters - Dr Hugo Brandenberger, the owner and head of the Biotta Company. For it was he who put it all together and created what Biotta is today.

What an interesting man he proved to be as we discussed his principles and practices, whilst a lighted candle burned to the side of his desk. A devout Christian, he has it there to always remind him of the Great Light which is ever present.

I found him an intriguing character whose name belied his diminutive physical presence, but in no way his extraordinary sense of purpose. Clearly it was this strong and forceful character which had determined Biotta's success.

When I asked how it all began he told me he was working for a large company, Knorr, but had the entrepreneurial flair to do his own thing. This smallholding in Tagerwilen, as it was in 1961, seemed to be just the answer.

"I have a principle" he told me "to serve only the best for a modest price - win the confidence of the consumer - then the profits will come".

It did seem to me that he had so effectively applied a fundamental rule that the unselfish motive of giving a service is a sure way of success, together with its rewards. Contrary to the conventional function of business where profit is the prime incentive and everything else is a means to this end. This latter policy usually concludes with a faceless organisation of monolithic proportions, topped by power hungry individuals and lower echelons, ever fearsome of their particular position on the rung of the ladder. Each with one eye over their shoulder to avoid the inevitable knife in the back. Not the best of surroundings to spend a third of one's life. Nor indeed particularly productive or of value to society. None of this was applicable to the family business of Dr Brandenberger.

"The maximum number of people working here will be eighty" he continued. "That allows only three levels - the workers, the supervisors and myself. If it gets bigger I have to introduce another level then I lose touch with the workers and that must never happen."

"One cannot serve the consumer without serving the employee" he added.
"I cannot change the world, but I can the place where I am living" he concluded. Such was his philosophy of life and it shone through his family, the supervisors and the workers, all of whom were clearly enjoying their life at work - close to the land and its produce.

There is something very satisfying being at one with the soil and its gifts. These people knew this and I was feeling it too.

"You are happy" boomed the smiling Willi Egli. I don't know if it was a question or an order, but I was! As originally a city dweller it was nice to be that close to nature.

It was Dr Brandenberger who took the vegetables growing a stage further.

Usually when nature wants to preserve something it introduces lactic acid fermentation so that the resulting lactic acids destroy all the harmful germs and decaying bacteria. The food does not purify and become poisonous, it turns to lactic acid. Two examples of this are genuine yoghurt and sauerkraut.

I can remember years ago experimenting with this very point for the benefit of my children with a jar of genuine yoghurt and a bottle of pasteurised milk. Left over a period of three days in normal temperature the yoghurt went sour but was edible. The milk went rotten and smelled revolting.

Such is the value of natural preservation. It was this lactic acid system which Dr Brandenberger turned to advantage in preserving his fruit and vegetable juices. But with a difference. Whilst the vitamins and natural enzymes present in the organic juices remain preserved and even enhanced in value, the fermentation of the lactic acids in the juice would and did impair the taste. So Biotta developed the lactic acid concentrate fermentation method which, when added to the juices, preserves them without changing the natural taste and flavour of the fruit or vegetables. This also gave them another advantage. For not only do the juices benefit from preservation of the nutritional aspects of the fruit or vegetable, but they are fortified by the mineral salts and trace elements of the concentrate.

On the subject of lactic acid, this is used in the Bio-Quick Test to establish whether a vegetable has been produced by organic or non-organic methods. The speed of growth of the lactic bacteria is the determining factor.

There are other tests nowadays which will differentiate between the systems of agriculture. For instance, the Light Emission Test uses radiation levels between biological and conventionally produced specimens.

There are enzyme tests and tests using thin layer and gas chromatography.

The prevention test is an interesting one, since organic vegetables do not lose as much water and in consequence remain fresher longer.

There is one more observation to be made about lactic acid which was culled from a book called *Fight Cancer* by Dr J Kuhl - "Lactic acid products specifically aid the cure and protection against chronic illness and, therefore, help to prevent cancer. Countries such as China, Russia, Bulgaria and Rumania prove this due to the large consumption of such products daily. Tumours can disappear within six weeks of intensive consumption. Continuing to eat lactic acid products prevents illness recurring (cases were watched for five years). Consumption of products without lactic acid and containing enzymes, even raw vegetables, do not cure. Cancer diseases of the tongue, skin, womb and vagina only react to treatment with lactic acid food. We would return to a healthy society if we all ate organically grown food. If we ate more lactic acid products there would be few cancer cases".

JUICE THERAPY

Raw fruit and vegetable juices have always been used and recommended in natural medicine as part of the healing system for many ailments and chronic diseases.

Generally speaking a juice diet will play an important role in stomach and intestinal conditions. It will benefit sufferers of such problems as cramp and inflammation and will act favourably in conditions affecting the liver, gall bladder, pancreas, urinary system and abdominal organs. Juices will relieve pressure on the heart and blood circulation and they can have a calming influence on the nervous system.

Perhaps the raw juice diet can be seen at its best when a cleansing or purifying diet is called for.

There is a rule of thumb, not altogether accurate, but sufficiently so to form a reasonable guide - that the cleansing foods grow high above the ground, cleansing and nourishing just above the ground, and nourishing foods below the ground.

In normal diet it is a balance of these which keeps one healthy. Which is why practitioners of natural dietetics will insist that an ideal daily diet comprises a fruit meal, a raw salad meal and a meal of conservatively cooked vegetables to include two green and one root vegetable. So when a person wants to lose weight quickly for instance, a diet based on raw fruit juices would be ideal, because these juices are cleansing. This would suit older people and the chronically ill, for a limited period, if supplemented with vegetable juices which are nourishing and easily assimilated.

The physiological process which takes place when one is hungry is that the metabolic system tends to turn acidic and the body protein is broken down along with some mineral loss. The introduction of raw fruit juice will neutralise this acidic condition as a result of its highly alkaline mineral content and this helps in the process of the excretion of the harmful acids occurring in the system. As with any diet for any ailment, elimination is of fundamental importance.

CHAPTER SEVEN

ASSIMILATION VERSUS ELIMINATION

The switch of emphasis from assimilation in a fasting situation, with or without a juice regime, to one of elimination, cannot be more earnestly stated. To enter into a cleansing programme without taking specific measures to ensure all eliminative channels are open and functioning is, to say the least, foolhardy. Over the course of years one's body accumulates small or large quantities of waste and toxic matter, depending on one's way of life.

Those who have given little or no consideration to their diet and other habits will naturally carry the heavier burden of these waste deposits.

I wrote earlier of the traces of DDT which accumulated in the fat tissues. All drugs, antibiotics, vaccines and sera will leave deposits in and around the body. The liver itself will at any time be performing a detoxifying role. Were it not to do so those toxic substances released into the bloodstream could poison the host! One has but to consider alcohol as an instance. Should the alcohol reach the bloodstream in only a small quantity in its original state, the person would surely die. It is in instances where the liver has reduced functioning ability as a cirrhosis, that one witnesses a physical breakdown of the body, as hugh amounts of toxic matter reach the bloodstream and which subsequently poison the cells.

It is important to understand this principle, because as the cleansing process proceeds, various reactions may occur which sometimes may not be very pleasant.

It is not unusual in citrus juice fasting, supplemented with herbs to detoxify the bowel, liver and kidneys, for the patient to eliminate via the bowel more than ten pounds of waste matter in two or three days. And that is without a single morsel of solid food entering the mouth during this period.

That often occurs with people who profess not to be constipated because they have a bowel movement daily. I fully understand the old pioneers of Nature Cure who used enemas, colonics and high colonic irrigations as part and parcel of cleansing and healing programmes. It does not occur so much today because there is a school of thought which considers it to be rather unnatural.

However, one can produce just as good results with the use of herbs, even though it may take a little longer.

Bowel cleansing is absolutely essential in any therapeutic programme. Unless one is prepared to accept this and ensure at least two, and better still three, movements daily then the real vitality and feeling of well being which comes as a result of cleansing will not be achieved.

On the continent many practitioners recommend the use of Glaubers salts. These have a purgative action and are undoubtedly very effective. Taking Glaubers salts should commence immediately before beginning a raw juice fast. Three teaspoons in three quarters of a litre of warm water to be taken by mouth over a period of twenty minutes. About two hours later evacuation occurs and may last on and off for several hours. Following this protracted evacuation raw juices may be taken. I prefer the herbal approach, since this is far more gentle in its effect and may be taken once, twice or three times daily in an amount to meet the unique needs of each person. My own favourite herbal combination, which has been used by untold numbers of patients and has stood the test of time, was passed down to me by the man who taught me traditional Nature Cure. It has never failed a single patient over the last sixty years or more.
Its formulation has an interesting history in that my mentor had gone through the whole gamut of dietary aids to find a 'universal solvent' capable of dealing with constipation once and for all for everyone. Like so many before him he had used onions, prunes, figs, senna, bran and other similar substances. Whilst each one would have an effect on some people, there was not one which would work for all people.

Then one day he was passing a field of cows and he saw how they evacuated. "That's it" he exclaimed. "That is how the human bowel should behave". Soft and pliable. No straining, pushing or forcing. And he immediately realised it was to the herbs of the field that he had to look to for his 'universal solvent'. He found it by experimentation and thus created his own special formula, a mixture of many herbs, each performing a particular function for cleansing and stimulating the liver, cleansing the bowel, acting on the kidneys so that these vital cleansing and excretory organs have the material which help them to work efficiently. Today there are similar herbal preparations sold in health food shops which one may take as often as needed without any harm. In fact only good can result because of their natural cleansing action.

People have often suggested that it could become habit forming. And I have replied that there are always habits - our lives are based on habit - what we eat and drink - when we eat and drink - what we think - how we behave - the important point is whether it is a good habit or a bad habit.

And there is no doubt that from a health point of view that this can only be a good habit.

It has always been a mystery to me that people give so much attention to eating and drinking and almost none to its elimination.

It is a salutary thought that nature sought fit to provide two entrances, mouth and nose, for assimilation of nutrients to serve the function of the human machine, but no less than five to ensure elimination occurs - bowel, bladder, skin, mouth and nose. This does seem to suggest elimination is more important than assimilation. And I remember it once being said - better to eat white bread and have three bowel movements daily than eat wholemeal bread and be constipated!

So, whether one is fasting or eating and living life normally, always treat elimination with the same thought daily as one would give to a meal.

CHAPTER EIGHT

THE ORGANIC JUICES
Carrots - Daucus carota

It has been said many times by the most eminent of natural healers throughout the annals of unorthodox publishing that the carrot is the most valuable of all the root vegetables.

However, one must say immediately that this is only so if the carrot has been grown organically. Carrots unfortunately are susceptible to any chemical that has been used in either fertiliser or pesticide or, indeed, detergents used in the cleansing process. So one must always choose carrots which are produced organically and therefore free from all the man made harmful residues used in commercial agriculture.

Carrots are one of nature's finest alkaline foods and when consumed raw have the ability to revitalise the intestinal flora. So many people suffer today from what one may describe as putrefied intestines, when this valuable organ should be clean and free of longstanding and decomposing fermenting waste. Much of the cause of this must be laid firmly at the door of antibiotics. The over use of this so called miracle of modern medicine has, in many instances, cleared the intestine of most of the natural intestinal bacteria which should be present at all times to break down and detoxify the body wastes.

A word or two now about carrots as a source of Vitamin A. Carrots do not contain Vitamin A per se. The yellowy orange colour is known as carotene which is converted to Vitamin A when ingested by the body. Carotene is, therefore, sometimes described as pro-Vitamin A, the substance capable of being turned into Vitamin A.

Nowadays whenever one speaks of Vitamin A the question of overdose is raised. This really is a great pity because the possibility of overdosing on Vitamin A from a vegetable food source is virtually impossible. Even when the source is from a high pro-vitamin A liquid like carrot juice there is simply no basis of fact that an overdose can occur. One may drink litres of carrot juice daily and derive nought but great benefit. It is true that the skin may slightly discolour, but I am convinced that this has little to do with the carrot or the carotene colour, but more to do with its beneficial effects on the liver. I say this because the principle has been tested by first removing the colour pigment before consumption and it still occurs. Also, were the former to be true and it was the carotene colour, then, surely, one would expect the colour of other foods to also affect the skin. And since many wholefood and vegetarian is laden with the natural green of chlorophyll, they should be looking quite green!

Another strong colour is that of the beetroot. Even those with a particular liking for this lovely vegetable do not actually reveal the signs of their liking with an over red skin!

Organic carrot juice has a cleansing effect on the liver and one may witness the release of clogged material which may have been retained for many years. Because this happens quickly and in considerable volume, depending on the individual, the normal urinary and intestinal channels are unable to cope with this overflow, so the body uses the next available channel of elimination via the lymph system and ultimately through the pores of the skin.

So any sign of colour does no more than indicate that the juice is giving the liver a good clean, which should be viewed most favourably. In any event, it disappears quite quickly once the cleaning of the liver is complete.

Having eradicated the false allegations which are too often aimed at carrot juice consumption, let us now consider the real advantages of taking organic carrot juice therapeutically or as part of ones normal and everyday diet.

It is not by chance that one of a baby's first solids is sieved carrots, because carrots are rich in most of the mineral elements, particularly calcium, which lays down the foundation for healthy bones and teeth. This is why naturopathic practitioners will prescribe organic carrot juice during a pregnancy and whilst lactating, thus improving the quality of the breast milk. A half to a bottle of Biotta Carrot Juice would be the order of the day on these occasions.

Carrot juice has an antiseptic action and is a must when one is prone to infections of any kind - throat, sinuses, any part of the alimentary canal, including the intestine when colitis occurs.

It is a most useful dietetic aid in treatment of blood poisoning, poor circulation and especially ulcerations. Certain eye conditions respond better when there is a daily dietary intake of carrot juice. Conjunctivitis particularly. Carrot juice does nourish the optic system as may be seen when it is introduced in quantity.

Skin conditions - eczema, psoriasis and simply dry skin will improve with the addition of organic carrot juice. And it is called for in nervous conditions too.

No wonder it has been described as the miracle food. Much of it due in scientific terms to its valuable content of many of the vitamin B group, vitamins C, D, E, the blood coagulant Vitamin K and so many of the important minerals - potassium, sodium, calcium, iron, magnesium, manganese, phosphorus, copper, chlorine and zinc.

It is said that we are all conditioned by our experiences through life, and that at any stage we are no more or no less than the sum total of this conditioning. We act in our daily responses to life according to this conditioning - that which we have learned and which has impinged on our consciousness - good and bad. It is an interesting concept which over years of investigation, observation and awareness in myself and others I have never been able to fault.

It was no surprise to me, therefore, that when I planned to write this book I should recall an item read over thirty years ago which gave me the insight into the healthy value of juices. I remember it well, for it had such an effect on me that it was to influence my thinking for most of my life.

It was the story of a girl who had lived on a farm in America and ate the usual refined, starchy, fatty, meaty diet until she married early in life. A car accident in her late twenties started a chain of events of 'nerves', jaundice, gall bladder disease resulting in her normal weight of ten stones diminishing to under five stones at which she was diagnosed as having splenic leukaemia.

I suppose to some extent I had identified her problem with my mother's who had also, as a result of liver disease, been obliged to reduce her weight by over half from thirteen and a half stones to six and a half stones.

This young lady had gone the usual rounds of doctors, specialists and clinics before she took the 'alternative' route and was prescribed a diet of carrot juice only. Firstly only in spoonful sips because she had little or no control over the bodily functions. Gradually this was increased to half a pint daily. Ultimately she was drinking no less than eight pints a day and nothing else at all. No other food, liquid or medication was taken for one and a half years! By which time all the depression symptoms, bowel haemorrhages, painful joints and lethargy had gone. Ten years later when I read the story she was fit and well and living a normal life. To Dr Kirschner who wrote the story and the one below I owe a real debt, because it was he who first showed me the value of juice therapy.

He also wrote about a little boy who, at the age of two and a half years, weighed sixteen and a half pounds. He was diagnosed as being allergic to milk and all animal products. The child's parents could find nothing, food or medicine, which would help the child who was by now very weak. That was until they tried carrot juice and other raw juices, supplemented with a little honey. This child grew to six feet and a healthy young man.

I had cause to remember this story some seven years later, for in 1963 our second child was born, and he was also allergic to milk - breast milk, cows milk, goats milk and even soya milk.

My early years of Nature Cure training were being put to the test I thought as I watched my wife struggle to breast feed him. The primordial urge to suckle was there. It was the body which was rejecting the nourishment, and she would reach for the bowl to catch the contents of the 'feed' as the lot was violently brought back. Feed after feed, day after day. This went on for weeks as my distraught wife had her milk analysed - perfectly normal - and tried cows milk, goats milk and soya milk - all to no avail.

Then I remembered the story I had read in Dr Kirschner's book,- Live Food Juices. This was the real test. No theory, but the actual practice on our own baby who was but a few weeks old.

We started with minute quantities of carrot juice, orange juice and grape juice. They stayed down. It was working. So systematically the quantities were increased over the weeks and months until supplemented with sieved vegetables. When my wife and I became vegetarians in the mid 1950's we had not anticipated that it would be so total as it was to be at the birth of our second son. Today he is a strong healthy five feet six inch man who still shuns milk. "Cows milk is for calves!" he would say to anyone who tried to tempt him.

An article on carrot juice would not be complete without mention of the work of Dr Max Gerson and his natural methods for the treatment of cancer. Much has been written about his wonderful work which is now practised in many places throughout the world.

Dr Gerson had first learned the value of fruit in treating his own migraine condition with apples - nothing but apples. These were effectively detoxifying the liver and it was this which played a huge part in his formulation of what was to become the Gerson Diet.

He, like those before and since, recognised that an efficient liver function was vital for any real recovery from cancer to take place. His system calls for no less than two pints of carrot juice to be taken daily but that carrot juice must come from organic sources.

Many of the early pioneering works of natural dietetics bear no reference to the term 'organic'. This really stems from the fact that prior to the Second World War in 1939 farming, as it is today, with the use of artificial fertilisers and a whole host of pesticides, was unknown.

Most arable farmers used the rotation system for growing crops, leaving the land fallow for a year or two every few years. There was plenty of manure. And compost was the 'fertiliser' on most smallholdings and market gardens.

It is, therefore, important that the reader seeks only juice from organic sources. It has been given to me by one of the highest authorities in juice therapy that raw juices do not work unless the juice is made from fruits and vegetables free from chemicals.

Earlier it was mentioned that one of the valuable constituents of carrots is carotene or pro-vitamin A. It has been scientifically proven that Vitamin A from natural sources does help alleviate certain eye conditions.

When asked a question about carrots and carrot juice helping tired eyes and night blindness, Dr E Schneider explained that the effect is determined by the high carotene content of the carrot. Carotene is broken down into Vitamin A by the liver. And that 100g carrots contains 7.2mg of carotene. He suggested that lack of vitamin A is widespread despite a general assurance that normal food supplies sufficient quantities. Tests have shown that children need a long time before they can see properly after darkness or after a strong glare. This proves a vitamin A deficiency, he concluded. There are a number of other factors which may indicate a shortage of vitamin A - a thickening of the conjunctiva - the cornea showing signs of discolouration - dryness with frequent inflammation - eyelids sticking - and not least, the sensitivity to light.

There is a further need to increase ones carotene supply in this modern age, as a result of the television. Many people suffer with eye problems as a result of the effects of television.

It is said that television viewing uses as much as fifty times more vitamin A than normally required. This causes a weakness in the eyesight. Initially in twilight, and as the deterioration worsens, in darkness. This can lead to stress on the eye nerves, resulting in retinitis and other serious eye disorders.

Too little vitamin A may be the cause of much eye strain both at home and in the office. Anyone suffering from eye strain, headaches and nerviness (twitching) as their eyes become tired would do well to take a glass of carrot juice daily.

It is best to use carrot juice as the source of carotene because the carotene lies in the cellulose wall cells of the carrot. This is only released when the cell walls are broken down by chewing or cutting. And chewing is not always an efficient way of obtaining optimum amounts of carotene. This can only be assured when all the cell walls are broken down by juice extraction methods.

Carrot juice is the most effective and efficient means of providing vitamin A naturally.

Latest scientific research is now linking vitamin A as an aid to the prevention of cancer. And in particular skin cancer. Beta-carotene, as it is known in clinical circles, exists in two distinct chemical forms - the CIS and TRANS form.

All synthetic vitamin A comes in the TRANS form and is stored in the liver.

Natural beta-carotene contains both forms depending on it's source. The TRANS form as found in root vegetables converts to vitamin A. Whilst the CIS form circulates freely round the body and is not stored in the liver.

Clinical evidence suggests that the CIS version acts as a scavenger of free radicals, some of which are potentially harmful to the body. Free radicals are molecules formed in the body as a by-product of its metabolic processes. Free radicals may also occur in the system as a result of exposure to environmental pollutants, including carbon monoxide from vehicle exhausts, tobacco, drugs and alcohol. It is this cleaning up of the free radicals by the CIS form of beta-carotene which is interesting scientists, because of the link with degenerative diseases such as cancer.

It is currently being suggested that root vegetables such as carrots contain the TRANS form, since roots are not subjected to the sunlight. Whereas the CIS form is found in the leafy vegetables such as cabbage, and this offers a form of protection from the sun's harmful rays.

It is this distinction which is leading to the mounting evidence that vitamin A will protect against skin cancer. It would seem clear that conventional or chemically grown juice is to be compared to synthetic vitamin A and organic carrot juice is the best natural source of beta-carotene.

Beetroot Juice - Beta vulgaris

After carrot juice the juice from the beetroot must be the next most used juice of all the root vegetables. This is mainly as a result of its value as part of the therapy for treating patients suffering from malignant growths.

Dr P G Seeger of Germany suggests that this is because it normalises the 'breathing' of tumour cells. And other researchers on the Continent have shown that there is a natural active anti-cancer substance in the beetroot.

One research project by Alexander Ferrenzi, who had eighteen years experience with the effects of beetroot on patients suffering from malignant tumours, had significant success. Of thirty eight patients tested, only two showed no improvement.

Sigmund Schmidt also carried out some research in general practitioners surgeries, where fresh beetroot juices and soured milk drinks such as yoghurt and quark produced satisfactory results in ninety cancer and twenty eight leukaemia patients. He explained that low blood pressure was normalised, appetite improved and pain disappeared. Life expectancy was lengthened.

Rudolf Breuss's patients also enjoyed this freedom from pain when they undertook his special cancer diet which I shall write about later.

Beetroot Juice is traditionally known for its action in building up the red corpuscles of the blood. Although the iron content is not particularly high compared with some other vegetables it is regarded as being easily assimilated.
This may be as a result of its amino acid content being of a favourable balance to help the chelation process. Perhaps a word

or two about chelation is necessary here. It is a process used naturally by the digestive system to ensure absorption of mineral elements.

Minerals such as iron, calcium, magnesium will not pass through the walls of the small intestine and then into the bloodstream unless they are enveloped by a particular combination of amino acids - a different combination for each different mineral element. These amino acids have to be present in the right number each time the mineral is consumed for absorption to take place.

That is why it is so important for minerals to be derived from their natural food sources, where nature in her wisdom has formed effective combinations.

The practice of orthodox medicine giving large quantities of iron to combat anaemia is certainly in line with the allopathic practice of using a sledgehammer to crack a nut. But in no way does it resolve the problem, as any poor unfortunate recipient will know. For it usually passes directly through the digestive system, turning the faeces black and hard, and severe constipation invariably results.

Manufacturers of mineral supplements are recognising this nowadays and many of their minerals have been 'chelated' by new and innovative techniques.

Nevertheless, the simplest form and most enjoyable method of taking organic minerals is by way of organic vegetable juice.

Whenever beetroot juice is discussed it usually leads to the problem many women suffer as a result of the menstrual cycle. The monthly loss of significant amounts of blood in many cases, should be supplemented by a six ounce combination of beetroot juice and carrot juice three times daily. Two parts carrot to one part beetroot is an ideal mix.

There is a reason for this, which I discovered some time ago. If beetroot juice is taken neat, so to speak, in any great quantity over the course of a day, it has a tendency to make one feel nauseated. It is probably because of its action on the liver. Anything which has a cleansing and, therefore, stimulating effect on the liver will often leave one feeling slightly sick. This happens whenever the liver is shaken up.

I always recall a practitioner colleague in Hove in Sussex around the mid century by the name of Captain Wilson-Jackson who, with military precision and charming brutality, would sit his liver patients astride a mechanical 'rocking' horse to stimulate the liver. Since its motion could be controlled it was not as bad a 'ride' as one may think. But I have never seen a patient get off looking as well as they did before they mounted this dreadful steed! Nonetheless, it served its purpose and got the liver working. Other practitioners are known to manipulate the liver into action, which likewise is not an experience one especially seeks!
After this, the relatively gentle action of pure beetroot juice is quite pleasant. Blended with carrot juice it is positively enjoyable.

Suffice to say those with efficiently functioning livers experience nothing but pleasure from an intake of this fine vegetable.

As women enter the menopausal period of their lives beetroot should again be considered. Just a few sips two or three times a day can be of real help and a great deal better than hormonal therapy with its prescription of synthetic chemical compounds complete with a variety of side effects, some known, but almost certainly dangers yet to be discovered.

There is another factor which causes some concern and that is the current preoccupation the pharmaceutical and health food industry has in promoting the consumption of calcium.

Since most of that which is offered in the form of tablets is derived from inorganic sources and is nothing more than chalk, it is doubtful that it does any good at all. Since little of it will be absorbed and that which is may form deposits in the blood vessels, thus causing a hardening effect of these blood routes, or placing an unfair burden on the heart by thickening the blood, leading to high blood pressure.

It is said that a woman entering the menopausal stage risks losing calcium from the bones. If this is a possibility then surely it is better that calcium be supplied to the system on a daily basis in an organic form by way of the juice of carrots and beetroot. Particularly when the sodium levels in beetroot will help in its breakdown for use by the cells.

I am convinced that the human machine, complete with self-preserving instinct, will not go to the trouble of breaking down calcium from bone if it is supplied on a regular basis in a ready to use form.

The biochemical experts will tell me I am over simplifying things. But I have implicit faith in nature and the body's ability to look after itself provided it is given the right material to work with.

That is not so say there is no case for calcium supplementation. Clearly there are many where it is necessary. But in these instances a supplement should be chosen which has a combination of calcium forms - citrate, lactate, carbonate, gluconate, chelated where possible, and with magnesium and other minerals and vitamins to ensure absorption.

Celery Juice - Apium graveolens

Celery juice might be described as nature's purifier. Both the stick and the knob celery are equally beneficial to health. Knob celery on the Continent is also known as celeriac, which is the root vegetable. And I noticed when I visited the Biotta factory to see them making juice that they use celeriac. It was unbelievable how much juice they could extract from these large hard and dry looking roots. Such is the mystery of nature that it preserves these precious juices deep in the fibrous cells. And precious is a good word to describe celery juice, particularly for those who suffer from rheumatism. In all nature's depository there is no finer remedy. Its effect comes from its very high content of natural organic sodium.

This sodium is not to be confused with the inorganic sodium chloride which we know as common salt. For this common table salt is responsible for deterioration of the kidney function, varicose veins, hardening of the arteries and other problems of the circulatory system.

Here again one has to distinguish between the product of nature and the product of the chemist's laboratory. If one listens to the chemist there is always confusion, because he will tell you sodium is sodium whatever its source. In much the same way as the use of the word ascorbic acid for describing vitamin C. The pharmacist will rightly say ascorbic acid is ascorbic acid whether it comes from an orange or is made synthetically in a laboratory and, therefore, there is no difference. So he will use the laboratory sample in concentrated form because it is both cheaper and more convenient, and call his product vitamin C. In truth he has stated the facts. But when we, who care about sourcing our nutrition from the plants and seeds of nature, talk about these nutritional substances, we mean something more, because they are something more. They are a carefully harmonised balance of food substances contained in particular plants for a purpose. Man's expertise would be better spent in producing and marketing these foods and persuading people to eat them in the right balance than isolating their so called 'active' ingredients so they may be synthetically produced in a factory.

There is, of course, one great argument which will ensure this will never happen - it is that one cannot patent a fruit or vegetable of nature. Therefore, the chemist cannot protect his product and thus he runs the risk of others producing the same thing. So he has no monopoly on the formula. And it is this which makes the money in the pharmaceutical industry. There is no profit in spending vast sums of money advertising and promoting a piece of celery or an orange. What you do if you are a profit motivated pharmaceutical house is to extract the active ingredient of celery or ascorbic acid from oranges, synthesise them, apply for a patent, and make your fortune!

And so a gullible, unsuspecting public is persuaded by much advertising and publicity that this tablet or that capsule, this synthetic formula or that laboratory produced combination is better than the original whole substance from which it was cribbed.

Do not be misled - food is the source of our nutrition and only those substances which are genuinely of plant origin, as close to their natural form as conceivably possible, should be sought.

This is why I am so keen to encourage the consumption of organically grown juices, because they are simply concentrated vegetables, free from the less easily digested fibrous matter, and truly a natural source of these elements so important to ones health.

The art is in choosing those which do one most good and suit the body's needs. And these needs do change from time to time.
The person whose diet is based on concentrated proteins and carbohydrates, the sugars and starches will, if there are inherent factors, be predisposed to endure the problem of rheumatism or any one of many diseases associated with this acid forming diet.

Obviously a change of diet is advocated so the over consumption is balanced with more vegetables and fruit.

And it is easy to use celery juice for immediate results. It is remarkable how quickly this will act.

Why? Because of its sodium content. For this mineral in its organic form performs two main functions - firstly it maintains the fluid balance of blood and lymph, thus preventing it becoming too thick and viscous.

Secondly it keeps calcium in solution. We have discussed earlier the essential function of calcium in the body's system - but this calcium, like sodium, must be derived from organic sources.

The problem with much of the calcium consumed is that it is converted into its inorganic form by the cooking process. Then it becomes insoluble in water and thus cannot be used to nourish the cells and tissues. So one's system becomes bound up with this useless material, laying down the foundation for all sorts of problems from arthritis, heart disease and haemorrhoids to kidney stones, stones in the gall bladder and varicose veins.
It is unfortunately a cumulative problem, so a continuing diet of

cooked carbohydrates and heavy proteins, red meats, cheese, eggs, can only make matters worse.

However, there is an answer to all this which lies in the regular daily consumption of organic celery juice.

In the case of rheumatism, celery juice will combat the build up of uric acid in the system and a reduction in the pain will be evident after a few days. A combination of two parts celery to one part carrot will change the taste if celery on its own is too strong. A small glass should be sipped three times daily before meals.

Where arthritis is present this too requires celery juice.

The importance of organic sodium in the diet cannot be over emphasised and it would surely be of benefit to almost everyone to take at least one small wine glassful daily.

Carbon dioxide will be eliminated more easily from the body when sufficient organic sodium is present. This is of real value to those who are unfortunate enough to live and work in smoky atmospheres.

The high magnesium levels found in celery juice have an excellent effect on nervous diseases and when combined with carrot juice can help protect the nerve sheath.

The iron present will help oxygenate the blood cells. So do remember organic celery juice when the acid forming problems occur - rheumatism, gout, arthritis, kidney problems, and heartburn.

If you are in need of a diuretic then celery juice is the answer.

And whether you are fit or unfit, if the weather is hot, try a glass of organic celery juice and watch everyone around you perspire while you keep dry and comfortable. Then you will know how celery juice can work on the body.

Potato Juice - Solanum tuberosum

Without doubt the potato must be the most used and well known vegetable of them all. It is just so unfortunate that its real merit is lost in its preparation for eating. For much of the goodness is lost.

However, before this is discussed there are two statements which need to be made.

First potatoes should only be eaten if they are organically grown and properly stored.

Second it is a misconception that potatoes are fattening. It is primarily the addition of butter or margarine to boiled or jacket potatoes, basting fat on roast potatoes and oil on fried and sauté potatoes which leads to excess weight, these being the most popular methods of cooking.

Potatoes grown by commercial methods as opposed to organic are subject to all sorts of chemical fertilisers and insecticides. In some instances the foliage is treated with a weak solution of cyanide substance to break it down, thus making it much easier to pick the potatoes.

The problem is, all the chemicals seep into the soil and much must be absorbed by the potato and tends to lie in or just below the skin. It is for this reason and the fact that they seem to be an ingredient of most main meals that commercially produced potatoes are not recommended.

There is another factor which can cause concern. That is the use of sprout inhibitors during storage.

Potatoes will develop sprouts under most storage conditions unless they are chemically treated. And since potatoes have to be picked at their best, and in temperate climates will only crop once a year, it inevitably means they have to be stored. In order to avoid sprouting they are normally dressed with a dusting of a chemical sprout inhibitor. It has even been known for organically grown potatoes to be subjected to this method! Which tends to defeat the purpose of growing by organic methods. Although the caring organic grower will ensure his potatoes are stored in temperature controlled storage facilities where a level can be just below that which will encourage sprouting.

It is unfortunate that potatoes have to be cooked before eating, since this undoubtedly robs much of the nutritional value. Where the potato is peeled then it is fairly certain there is little in the way of vitamins and minerals left. The end result is mostly starch.

The real benefits of the potato are best obtained by turning it into juice. But this juice must be from potatoes grown only by organic methods. Then one has a substance of great value, which lies in the potato's antispasmodic activity. It is a specific remedy for over acid stomachs.

The solanin and vitamin C influence this by their effect on the secretion of the stomach juices. Where ulcers are present the potato juice must be given over a period of time with a specially prescribed diet.

If it is simply a case of overproduction of acid along with the usual inflammatory conditions, then a few days, maybe three or four, on potato juice, followed by a diet of light foods, principally root vegetables which have been pulped to reduce the digestive process, is the solution.

In all instances of stomach acidity the juice should be taken immediately before a meal to achieve the best results. After a few days the burning sensation (heartburn) and pressure in the pit of the stomach will disappear.

Dr Habil and Dr Magerl of Heidelberg used organically grown potato juice in a test on twenty five hospital patients. Nineteen of these were long term hospital treated but with no success. Six were new patients. Only three showed no improvement. The rest reported no pain after only the second day of treatment. There was a weight gain and secretion was normalised by the conclusion of the test. For anyone suffering from this impleasant condition, be it an ulcer or over-acidity, and it should be said that the symptoms of over-acidity form the greater number of complaints, potato juice

really is a must. It is such a simple and effective remedy.
Unfortunately, raw potato juice does not suggest a very nice taste
to most people. However, I found the Biotta Potato Juice pleasant
to drink on its own, but the addition of one-third organically grown
carrot juice will satisfy all tastes.

Potato Juice is also an excellent cleanser and is particularly
effective for skin conditions. From blemishes to eczema, the juice
of raw potato can be of great value taken internally.

Interestingly this will only work with raw potato. Once the potato
or the juice has been cooked it does not have any effect. This is an
instance of how cooking will destroy the healing and, indeed,
nutritional properties of the foods we eat.

Take the juice on its own or flavoured with carrot or lemon juice
twice daily between meals.

Where there are signs of inflamed nerves or muscle such as is
found in lumbago, sciatica or gout, then all highly acid foods such
as meat, fish, coffee and highly sugared products must be
eliminated from the diet and a combination of equal
parts of potato, carrot and celery juice will be most beneficial.

Tomato Juice - Lycopersicum esculentum

Whilst the tomato is thought of as a vegetable, it is actually a berry.
And a very nutritious one too. But only if the fruit of the tomato
plant is ripened on the stalk.

The vitamin C content is significantly greater than tomatoes picked
green and ripened in the dark. This is obvious when one
understands all plants draw their vitality from the sun, and like
homo sapiens, the greater the vitality the better is the absorption of
nutrients.

This is probably one of the areas of human physiology which needs
developing. Although it is difficult to measure.

It was Dr Henry Lindlahr, a pioneer and teacher of natural

therapeutics, who said there is but one disease - lowered vitality. For it is only when this vitality is below par that one leaves oneself open to illness. External germs and viruses see the body as a breeding ground, because the bodily organs and systems are operating below the norm, so assimilation is partial and elimination is less than efficient.

Natural law suggests the same principle applies in all living things. And it may well be emphasised that the over fertilisation of the soil by the use of chemical fertilisers has an effect similar to man's abuse of such drugs as heroin, cocaine and the like. They cause an unnatural result, however pleasant at the time, which has to be balanced by a corresponding depletion with all its negative and depressing effects.

In order to keep the production going it then becomes necessary to keep up the 'fixes' with increasing doses until the vitality of the soil succumbs.

Looked at in that light it becomes plainly imperative that the organic method be universally adopted without delay.

This production problem may be carried a stage further. If the plants produced by this over-stimulating system, which clearly deprives the soil of much of its value, are consumed by man, then he likewise becomes less nourished. So he eats more, overtaxes his system by placing an unfair burden on the organs. They wear out too soon in an overweight body that cannot cope. Which is then subjected to medicinal drugs in an attempt to stimulate it into action to fight off the effects of some disease or other caused by the 'lowered vitality'.

It does seem that lemmings are not the only creatures bent on self destruction!

However, let us go back to the humble organic tomato which, more than most vegetables, yields a delicious and flavoursome taste unknown to its chemically produced counterpart.

Organically grown tomato juice is rich in vitamins and many minerals, including copper. The latter being most important in building up many enzymes. These have a beneficial effect on the heart and blood vessels and are, therefore, good for circulation.

It is known that the juice can lower blood pressure. It will also increase stomach and pancreas secretion and is a valuable help when dieting to lose weight.

Pure tomato juice may be consumed by diabetics, as tomatoes may be eaten in almost any quantity without harm.

The question is often raised as to the acidity of tomatoes. And this must be understood before choosing ones source of the vegetable or the juice and how they are combined with other foods.
The plant ripened organically grown tomato has an alkaline reaction despite its high content of citric, malic and oxalic acids. But this is only the case if it is eaten when there are no concentrated carbohydrates with the same meal. Tomatoes eaten with bread or potatoes, for instance, will give an acid reaction.

The natural acids present are valuable to the bodily system of digestion and metabolism, but only if raw and organic. Tomatoes and the juice when cooked or canned disturbs or changes the nature of these acids, which then can have a deleterious effect on ones health; although it may not necessarily be immediately realised. It is not unknown for stones in the bladder and kidneys to be the result of an over consumption of cooked or canned tomatoes, either as a vegetable or as a drink.

Organically grown tomato juice may be used on its own, or in combination with many other juices as a refresher or for therapeutic action. With the minerals calcium, phosphorous, potassium, manganese, iron, copper and cobalt present, it is an excellent source of nutrition - but for best results drink it on its own or with other vegetables; never sweetened and not with starchy food.

A delicious combination of tomatoes, carrots, celery and beetroot is provided in Biotta Vegetable Cocktail.

Radish Juice
- Raphanus niger-Raphanus album-Raphanus sativus

In Britain it is the pink radish which is mainly sold as a salad vegetable. On the continent of Europe the black and white radish is used, depending on the seasons.

During my visit to the Biotta factory in Tagerwilen I was told they use only the black and white variety when making radish juice.

Rudolf Breuss insists the black or white radish must be used for making his special vegetable juice blend.

Whichever one uses, depending on the time of year, there is a word of warning - never take radish juice on its own. It is far too strong in its effect. And for this reason it is best to add a little beetroot juice to taste or water as desired. Do not, however, let this warning put you off the juice, which is bottled for its therapeutic and nutritive value, as are all Biotta organic juices.

Probably its greatest value is in emptying the gall bladder. So in biliousness radish juice is an excellent remedy.

In Switzerland, under test conditions, using sound and X-rays, it was possible to see how an intake of radish juice contracts the gall bladder.

A glass of organically grown radish juice taken before every meal can prevent and alleviate gall bladder problems. Start with just a tablespoonful before each meal. Then gradually increase, if well tolerated, up to a small wineglass.

According to Dr Schneider in Switzerland, if radish juice is taken regularly for months and the patient chooses a healthy life style, gall bladder complaints can be completely cured. Radish Juice will have a stimulating effect on the bowel too, thus encouraging better evacuation. In fact it influences the whole metabolic system from the stomach through the liver, gall bladder and intestinal tract; it has an effect on the fluid content through its high alkalinity, thus benefitting kidney and bladder function. And its action on the respiratory system deserves particular mention.

Radish juice has great beneficial action on the mucous membrane, and in conjunction with a puree of horseradish, can clear the accumulation of mucus in the sinuses. Which, by any measure, is far less painful and inconvenient than an operation to drain them. If the patient would then refrain from a diet with an excess of milk and starchy, sugary foods, the complaint would be cured for ever.

This is an old Nature Cure remedy. And it works on the basis of the horseradish dissolving the accumulated and hardened mucus, whilst the radish juice clears it from the system.

Take just half a teaspoon of fresh finely grated horseradish to which should be added enough fresh lemon juice to keep it moist, twice daily, morning and afternoon between meals. Nothing must follow it, either liquid or food for a few minutes after it has been taken.

The effect initially will be to cause lots of tears, the patient having first become aware of a sensation in the head. This effect will be to a greater or lesser degree, depending on the severity of the condition.

As the treatment progresses over weeks or even months, the sensation will disappear. At that stage you will know the mucus has been dissolved and cleared.

One hour after the horseradish has been taken, a small wineglass of organically grown radish juice and carrot, mixed half and half, should be slowly sipped. This will help cleanse the system of the accumulated mucus and restore and tone the mucus membrane lining.

Radish juice must always be taken diluted and in small quantity. It is an effective treatment for all mucus membrane conditions where there is an accumulation of phlegm, including bronchial asthma.

The Natural Antioxidant Cocktail

It has always been my simple premise that the difference between health and disease lies in the balance of foods consumed. And rather than use the standard guide of protein, carbohydrates, fats my rule of thumb is whether the food is cleansing, nourishing or congesting.

In those three words are all the individual nutrients that the scientists have identified and named which have since been built into a complex and consumer confusing maze by well intentioned and concerned nutritionists.

Obviously over time many foods have become known as a particularly good source of this vitamin or that mineral. A knowledge of which foods contain what, useful though that may be, does not on its own resolve how much we should eat of one food in relation to another, even though authorities have fixed what are euphemistically known as RDA's (Recommended daily amounts). These, incidentally, vary from country to country, each making up their own, even though climates and conditions are often similar. So it is anybody's guess what is the right level of any particular constituent and food for homo sapiens, especially as its benefit is ultimately based on each individual's ability to absorb and utilise the nutrients it contains.

It is human nature to think that if a certain vitamin potency does us good then a greater quantity will be even better. We know to our costs that there are limits to this theory, indeed too much may be poison to the body! Too little and deficiencies arise.

However, there is no one and only formula to meet people's needs. But history and modern science has taught us that there are lower and higher levels of vitamins and minerals beyond which problems of deficiency and toxicity respectively can arise.

This would not normally be a problem for man where a good diet and digestion with an efficient absorption system is evident, since all the nutrients required may be obtained from the food consumed.

We live in a world which is obsessed with analysing and breaking down everything to its individual particles in order to associate this or that function or disease with too much or too little of a particular element.

However, there is another way, and for that one must go back to my simplistic breakdown of foods - that is, cleansing, nourishing and congesting.

Generally speaking the cleansing foods are the fruits - nourishing foods are vegetables and everything else is more or less congesting. This food category is based on Nature Cure practice, in that the naturopath will use these foods in the diet in direct proportion to how fast or slow he judges the body needs to return to a healthy condition without imposing too great a burden on the patient. To cleanse too quickly will release too many toxins from bodily deposits into the system and cause any number of uncomfortable conditions - failure to remove too much of the congesting foods from the diet will simply slow down progress as the body adds to an already toxic overload which has caused the illness in the first instance!

A level of nourishing food is necessary in order to supply basic nutrients. By careful observation of the patient, an understanding of these basic dietetic principles and application of the right combination will restore most of the unhealthy to vibrant health.
A healthy diet comprises 75% fruit and vegetables, 10% protein (nuts, meat, cheese, eggs, fish), 10% carbohydrate (starchy and sugary foods), 5% fat (vegetable [preferably] or animal) - that surely is what should be the norm. A very, very small percentage of people consume such a diet, hence an overburdened health service!
As I write the media tells us we should be eating five pieces of fruit per day. I would say the amount of fruit we eat has to be in relation to the rest of the dietary intake to have any effective and positive impact on ones health.

The balance needs to be maintained. The person whose diet is overly protein, starch and fat food would need to eat a field of vegetables and an orchard of fruit to compensate and maintain a balance. It is simpler to reduce the protein, starch and fat foods to bring them into line with the fruit and vegetable consumption.

In other words, when meal planning one should start by choosing the fruits and vegetables, then add the proteins, starches and fats.

A wide variety of foods should be chosen, as much of it organically produced as is possible. Then the individual food nutrients necessary to meet bodily needs will be met.

Today there is much talk of the value of the antioxidant nutrients - vitamins A, C and E for instance.

These vitamins protect against the damaging substances in the air we breathe, the water and food we consume, which lead to excessive numbers of damaging particles in our body, collectively known as free radicals. These have a damaging effect on the cell structure by causing oxidation or decomposition. This creates what is described by experts as 'oxidative stress' which, in turn, leads to a weakening of the immune system.

It obviously follows that an inefficient system of immunity leaves the body vulnerable to all the poisonous man made and natural toxins which are an inevitable part of our daily living. To supply the body with the protective elements available in nutritional form is absolutely vital. Failure to do so will almost certainly lead to a slow persistent breakdown of health until some chronic disease befalls us.

Science has identified the vitamin antioxidants. The first is beta-carotene, the vegetable precursor of vitamin A. This is found mainly in the yellow and orange vegetables and fruits like carrots, apricots and mangoes.

The body uses it to make vitamin A and will make only what it needs. This is important, because an excess of vitamin A in its pure form from animal sources can be toxic.

Many people take the view that the body should derive its vitamin A from the beta-carotene containing vegetables only and thus avoid any possibility of toxic excess.
Scientific studies have shown that the risk of becoming ill with circulatory problems, stroke and heart attacks as well as cancer, escalates if the beta-carotene intake is insufficient.

It has also been discovered that the average person has a beta-carotene consumption of about one quarter the recommended daily supply. This bears out the Nature Cure doctrine that most of our diet should compromise fruit and vegetables.

So much has been written about Vitamin C, but it deserves further mention because of its valuable antioxidant properties. Its function in supporting the body in its fight against the cell damaging free radicals is well known. And scientific evaluation of this important substance confirms that it activates the immune system and plays a decisive role in combatting cancer.

Vitamin C can be found in abundance in many fruits, including oranges, lemons and the soft fruits.

The third vitamin antioxidant is E, that elusive vitamin because it is found only sparsely in the regular western diet. Its best vegetable sources being wheat germ, soya and some lettuce.
Yet it is one of the most important vitamins for mankind. Heart attacks and strokes would be reduced by 20-30 per cent if a sufficient supply was taken daily - according to recent scientific evidence. Though this and much more was established by the brothers Doctors Evan and Wilfred Shute of Canada who, from the 1930's spent a lifetime studying the function and effects of vitamin E on the circulatory system.

When I found that the Biotta company had produced an organic juice containing these vital vitamins it provided the answer to a quest for a source of the antioxidants naturally in a simple live fruit and vegetable form as part of ones daily diet.

Every one of A, C and E vitamins are present in this juice in substantial amounts, for the sources are rich in them - an organic blend of oranges, carrot, beetroot, lemon, sea buckthorn, concentrated vitamin E in wheat germ oil, sweetened to taste with fruit sugar.

Just one decilitre of this marvellous fruit and vegetable juice cocktail before a meal will provide one third of the daily requirement. So here is a food which guarantees the total daily need if a small glass is taken three times daily.

That appeals because it is nature's way of providing those important nutrients which, in an age of pollution, tobacco and alcohol consumption and junk food, must be an imperative part of everyones diet if they wish to stay healthy.

For without a strong immune system to maintain a twenty four hour defence system against all the toxins of today's environment, it is inevitable that the body will succumb and become further weakened.

It is the immune system which is the body's health guardian, and its armamentarium is here provided in a natural fruit and vegetable juice, the most convenient and concentrated source of nutrition.

Rudolf Breuss in consultation

RUDOLF BREUSS AND HIS VEGETABLE JUICE DIET

Of all the organic vegetable juices produced by Biotta, there is little doubt that the Breuss juice has the most exciting history. Indeed many will say that it is the juice of the future.

Behind the name is an extraordinary story of one man's pursuit of a diet to arrest the onslaught of cancer, the modern scourge of mankind.

That man was Rudolf Breuss, an Austrian, who during his earlier years was as electrical engineer. Much of the time he worked in hospitals. The illness of others which he was able to observe first hand during his working hours, coupled with his own health problems, stimulated an interest to investigate alternative methods from those employed by orthodox medicine in the hospital where he worked.

Born in 1899, he was in his forties before he began his career change. And it was a simple German book written over four hundred years earlier which was to capture his attention and direct his work for the rest of his life. The book expounded the value and use of fruit and vegetable juices.

For some time he experimented on himself to find the right mixture and balance of juices to serve the purpose of providing just sufficient nourishment to keep a person alive over a period long enough to clear the problem, particularly cancer.

His hypothesis was simple. To orthodox medical thinking perhaps too simple. But it was to prove itself over and over again in so many cases during the thirty or more years he was in practice and indeed some ten years after until his death in his 91st year in 1990.

Today his system is still used in Britain, the European continent, America and many other countries of the world, by people seeking a more gentle alternative treatment to that offered by conventional medicine.

Rudolf Breuss maintained that cancer, wherever it occurs in the body, feeds and grows from protein. He therefore deduced that if one fasted for what has now been confirmed to be an ideal period of six weeks, during which various herb teas would be taken to detoxify, cleanse and eliminate, the cancer would starve and be absorbed and subsequently pass out of the body by one means or another.

What he sought was a selection of vegetable juices which would provide just enough nourishment to meet the basic requirements of the body during the six week period, but for all intents and purposes no protein, nor indeed the many and varied congesting foods which make up the normal diet.

The ultimate result was a mixture of organically grown vegetable juices comprising carrot, beetroot, celeriac, continental radish and potato. Not only was Rudolf Breuss meticulous in his instructions for making particular herb teas, he was with the vegetable juices too. Each one had to be a specific quantity in order to get the balance right. In the early days he prepared the juices himself. Then his patients did their own. To obtain all the vegetables from organic sources, even on the Continent, proved difficult, and such was the success of his treatment that the demand necessitated a more businesslike attitude to the problem. So he approached the Biotta company in Tagerwilen.

He gave them his formula. They made the juice exactly as he wanted it, using their tried and tested methods of preserving that life force in the juices which make all Biotta juices so beneficial.
Breuss then tried out the results on a number of patients to ensure it was as effective as freshly expressing it using a home juicer. It was. This was the breakthrough he needed, thus making it possible for people all over the world to use his system when suffering from cancer and other serious diseases.

When he reached the age of eighty he could no longer cope with the demands of sufferers on his time and he retired. In order that his methods should continue to be available he put his life's work into a book which was published first in German and subsequently in French, Italian, Serbo Croat and English.

My time with Rudolf Breuss was an extraordinary and very special experience. For here was a real healer. A man who had that gift, that instinct which made his diagnostic technique all appear so simple and easy.

I met many of his ex-patients who, in their own words, were all cured of various forms of cancer. The professor of music who at the age of fifty six suffered a brain tumour with a poor prognosis - an operation, a silver plate permanently in his head, a possibility of pain for the rest of his life and no guarantee of success. He chose instead to take the Breuss diet. He told me that after the third day the pain subsided and a few days later it went completely. After forty two days he was well. When I met him he was seventy four, some eighteen years after the event.

Then there was the owner of an Austrian health food store who was the first person to try Breuss's system. She had a cancer of the breast and would not have an operation because her mother had suffered terribly following a similar operation for the disease. She too had been cured and that was thirty two years before I met her!

Ten years prior to our meeting Frau Schelser had also suffered from breast cancer. At the age of fifty she was well and free of all problems. As was a delightful lady who ran a natural therapy clinic at the time with her husband, a microbiologist. She told me her husband photographed the changes taking place in her blood cells each week during her six week course. The effect of the vegetable juice and herb teas showed a distinct pattern of improvement as I was to see from the actual photographs.

I met a lady in her seventies who told me she had stomach and intestinal cancer in her early fifties and the Breuss method had cured it.

There were many more people during my stay who told me their stories of success. I wondered how much the presence and charisma of the healer influenced the healing process. For it is well known that a practitioner can and often does have a psychologically positive influence.

Rudolf Breuss took me to a cupboard and showed me thousands and thousands of neatly filed letters from people from all over Europe and other parts of the world. "I have not met these people" he told me. "They have simply followed instructions and have become well".

Clearly it was the diet which did the job as I was to see over the next decade or so in Britain. For publication of the book in English created much interest and still does. It has always been a great privilege for me to have met this compassionate Austrian healer and for the fact that I was given a unique opportunity to play a small part in his work and, of course, to learn from him.

Today, despite his passing, his work continues through his book which has so far sold 850,000 copies worldwide (English edition available at health food shops or direct from Nuhelth Books, 26 Church Street, Stroud, Glos GL5 1JL).

I must mention an interesting occurrence which proved to me the power and value Rudolf Breuss's Vegetable Juice has on the human system.

During my stay, I was to call on a well known naturopathic practitioner in Konstanz. "When you come bring a bottle of Biotta's Breuss Vegetable Juice with you" he told me. It was a funny request considering he uses and prescribes it all the time. However, I duly went along with his instruction and arrived, with my wife, at his practice one morning. "I see you brought the juice. Now who is going to take it so I can show you how it works?" he enquired. We decided my wife would, and he proceeded with us to a room where he had a special camera which photographs the rays or energy which emanate from the hands and feet. It is known as Kirlian photography and is used to illustrate visually what some people call the aura.

He had my wife sit in front of the machine and place her hands and feet on the plates in front of her. He flicked a switch and we awaited the photograph. He then opened the bottle of juice, poured a small amount into a clean glass and asked my wife to drink it slowly, being sure to mix each sip with her saliva before swallowing. "It will take about twenty minutes to work, so let me show you round" he said. And we followed him from room to room in his large and successful practice, arriving back in the original room some twenty minutes or so later. Again my wife went through exactly the same procedure and we awaited the result.

The difference between the before and after pictures was amazing. The strength of the rays in the second picture were much more powerful, pronounced and clearer.

"That is what Biotta's Breuss Vegetable Juice does for the body - it gives it that additional vitality." he added "Which is why I asked you to bring the juice yourself, because I know you may think I had done something to it if I had used my own. And that is also why I insisted your wife held on to the bottle whilst I was showing you round."

It was an impressive example the memory of which has stayed with me ever since. It also emphasised the message both Dr Hugo Brandenburger of the Biotta company and his 'man of the earth' Herr Willi Egli left with us when we were later visiting the Biotta plant. The message was not in words but in fact. It was their special relationship with, and deep respect for vegetable plants, the soil, the sun, air and water which nurtures them, together with the human contribution which ensures their value is not destroyed but remains vital until such time as the contents are consumed as a life giving and health protecting juice. For surely there is no other example today which provides so easily the vitamins, minerals, trace elements and enzymes to keep one healthy, than organically grown vegetable juices.

Rudolf Breuss's Vegetable Juice diet is, to my mind, one of the greatest gifts available to us. Taking it as a sole source of nutrition for forty two days for those serious conditions such as cancer is not easy. It requires great courage and determination because, for most people, a fast for such length is unheard of. It is a completely new and unexplored experience. However, many people, like the ones I met in Austria, have been restored to health by following it. They are the pioneers. And many many more will follow. But they have to have the necessary strength of character to meet the resistance put up by orthodox medical practitioners and well meaning relatives who feel surgery, radiotherapy and chemotherapy is the only way. Despite the very poor success rate, about 5% on average for the most common cancers, in relation to its use. Then there are the side effects - the nausea, loss of hair, depletion of vitality as the body's self preserving mechanism and organs endeavour to cope with the chemical onslaught.

It is true the orthodox methods do have their successes, at whatever the interim cost of suffering and the incapacity, and it is marvellous for those people, that average 5%. And I would not want to dissuade or preclude anyone from choosing that method if it is their wish. For it is one of the joys and lessons of life that we mostly have a choice in the decisions we make. The art of success is in making the right decision at the time. How can we be sure we have made the right decision initially in any given situation? That's the problem, we can't always. Because there are no certainties in this life, except its expiry! But mostly the decisions we make are not a matter of life or death or the possibility of permanent pain and suffering. Yet when the cancer diagnosis arises that is different. Here is the life or death situation and a decision must be made. How does one make the best decision? Indeed, can one make a reasoned decision without knowing all the possibilities?

It is unfortunate that the medical system operating in Britain, indeed in most countries, does not give the opportunity for other than the orthodox or allopathic methods to be presented to the patient. It is they who have usually diagnosed the disease and they who suggest the treatment. And since mostly they know only their own methods, it is those which prevail. So the sufferer never gets to hear whether there are any alternatives. If, however, they are inquisitive enough to seek other avenues and report back to their hospital consultant that a neighbour or friend suggested a fast or a specific dietetic change may be a first effort, one can hardly expect the consultant to be over the moon with the thought that his training, knowledge and expertise in his specialist field, accumulated over perhaps many years, is about to be usurped by a suggestion from an unqualified acquaintance of the sufferer.

So he usually, though not always, resorts to the 'time is of the essence' fear factor.   An operation or radiotherapy and/or chemotherapy 'must be done before it is too late'. And the sufferer succumbs. Sometimes that may be true, often not so. Usually there is time to review, even try the Breuss system as many testimonials in his book indicate.

That is why I believe Rudolf Breuss wrote in so much detail what his method is and how to undertake it. And why it is explained easily for people to follow. He wanted to give everyone an alternative opportunity which he knew had worked successfully for many people.

Over the last ten years or so I have heard of cases where doctors and consultants have shown, often at best, a passing interest when presented with the Breuss book by their patient and have given time for the patient to try the vegetable juice fast. They have also been very willing to monitor their health during the six weeks. And indeed have shown rather more interest when the patient has come through it successfully. This is particularly so in those cases where their original prognosis was 'I'm afraid there is nothing more we can do'.

So whilst I am not personally advocating everyone with cancer should abandon orthodox medicine in favour of the Breuss system, I am saying it can be of real value for some, a more gentle lifesaver for others and, not least, a last and sometimes surprisingly beneficial resort for those for whom the doctors medicine cannot help - those sent home to die.

However, don't simply think of Breuss's Vegetable Juice as only for the really serious problems. If it can help them, its value for many lesser ailments is inestimable.

CHAPTER TEN

THE USE OF VEGETABLE JUICE IN DISEASE

Much has been written about juice fasting. There are the advocates of water only. There is a good case for resting completely the organs of digestion.

Then there are those who maintain water and fruit juices are the best method. This method over a limited period can give real benefit as the cleansing action of the fruit takes effect. However, note must be taken of nutritional research, particularly that of Dr Ragnar Berg, which does suggest that the excessive acidity of the body increases so much that it loses its ability to breakdown the accumulated toxins. This fasting method can also be difficult for patients in the early days as a sense of ill-ease, of not being alert or feeling well, can occur.

It is true these fasting methods have their place, but care should be taken to ensure they do not become the one and only rule.

For instance, it would not be wise to fast a chronic rheumatism or arthritis case on citrus juices - their system could not take it as the normal acid to alkaline conversions would not take place. It would not be sensible for patients with kidney or heart problems to undertake a rigid fast on fruit juices.

Neither, of course, should highly nervous people. And fasting is out for people with tuberculosis for example. So, despite much written about the value of fasting, it is not a hit and miss therapy, it must be scientifically prescribed in strict accordance with the patients condition.

Sometimes water only. Sometimes water and fruit juices. But mostly, particularly for a long fast, the raw alkaline juices from vegetables is the answer.

The benefits of cleansing bodily toxins have been proven time and again with the use of vegetable juices.

Probably the most effective in our time is the Breuss Vegetable Juice fast.

This unique blend of carrots, beetroot, celeriac, radish and potato is taken in alternation with herb teas, for a fasting period of forty two days - six weeks with simply nothing other than glasses of the vegetable juice and cups of herb tea. No solid food at all. Yet this simple formula has the effect of breaking down and absorbing tumours.

This same blend may be used for all manner of diseases taken for a lesser period of fasting time or with food, depending on the severity of the condition.

Dr Johnnes Kuhl in Germany and Dr Max Gerson in America also recommended vegetable juice fasting. Though he died many years ago, the Gerson system has stood the test of time and is still available in many countries. Although it encompasses in total more than the simple vegetable juices, they are the basis of his and most other dietetic fasting methods for the treatment of serious conditions.

Ebba Waerland, whose husband Are Waerland gave his name to what is known as the Waerland System, advocated vegetable juice fasting, understanding that its effect was not only so good, but that the patients taking the fast enjoyed the feeling of well being, whilst the brain became alert and there were no real feelings of hunger after the first day or two.

The advantage of a therapeutic vegetable juice fast is that it keeps the body supplied with nutrients whilst the body's own resources are used in dealing with the diseased tissue.

Even where a disease is so advanced there is no hope of recovery, a vegetable juice diet, begun in time, will help the patient reach death without the trauma of pain which so often accompanies it

How to use the Juices

First and foremost it must be clearly understood vegetable juices are not drinks as such and should not be taken to quench ones thirst. For this pure water is best.

Therefore when taking vegetable juices, a small amount should be sipped and mixed with the saliva before swallowing. A period of ten to fifteen minutes is ideal when consuming a small wineglassful.

The quantity taken per day varies considerably according to the dietician and the problem. Rudolf Breuss urges cancer patients to take half a litre of his mixture a day, but never less than a quarter of a litre.

Ebba Waerland recommends about one to one and a half litres a day, providing there is no heart or kidney trouble. If there is, only up to three quarters of a litre per day is allowed.

Both the above examples are when fasting on vegetable juices without solids. Additional liquid if thirsty is usually water or herb teas.

When using juices as part of the daily diet then there is greater flexibility. Some juices may be consumed half a litre at a time, although so much at one sitting is a lot for the body to deal with. Other juices, like radish, must be diluted and only taken in sherry glass quantities at a time.

Remember, when taking vegetable juices they are assimilated in fifteen to thirty minutes. The same solid cooked or raw vegetables require hours to digest. So you get lots of nutrients quickly with little or no digestive effort on the part of the body. This is energy saving dietetics!

When preparing your own vegetables, be sure to wash them thoroughly and do not peel. That way you lose so much of their value. That is one reason why you must choose organically grown, free from residues of chemical fertilizers and insecticides.

Irradiation of foodstuffs is beginning to take place as yet another way is sought to preserve our food. Great care should be taken to avoid anything which has been treated by this method, since there is enough information already to suggest it alters the molecular structure of the food, and certainly reduces its nutritional value.

Since it is unlikely organic fruit and vegetables would be subjected to this process, it is yet another good reason for choosing this whole food produce.

Choosing organic food for consumption is a sure way of avoiding genetically modified plant material - science's latest interference with nature for commercial gain with complete disregard for the consumer.

In fact, there is considerable evidence accumulating that the pollution of our food is the cause of so much illness and suffering it is a pity that legislators have not taken action to protect the public. But when you consider the vested interest of the chemical industry and the giant food conglomerates and their money generating capacity, it is not at all surprising that consumer health is not a priority! However, that is another story.

The best advice I can give is take a serious responsibility for your own health by searching out only those foods which are grown and produced naturally. Eat as much raw fruit and vegetables as possible, and be sure they represent seventy five per cent of the total diet. Then barring accidents and adverse inherent factors (even the latter can sometimes be improved), one may live a life free from the many and various ailments which humanity appears to impose upon itself.

If that seems to be a sweeping statement, all I can say is try it and see for yourself. It has worked for too many people for it to be simply the luck of the draw.
Start with the organic vegetable juices for they contain valuable nutritional substances and that special essence of life which ensures a healthy cellular structure throughout the body, which yields the ultimate protection - an inbuilt resistance to disease and a vibrant vitality.

There is no example so plain as the work of Rudolf Breuss, the Austrian herbalist who devised his own juice formulae for cancer and other serious diseases.

THERAPEUTIC USES OF VEGETABLE JUICES
- A BRIEF SUMMARY

BEETROOT JUICE - 1 wineglass daily.

Too much may cause nausea or dizziness. Mix with carrot for a tastier juice and to remove that problem.

- Ideal for its building and toning properties.

- A must in any dietary cancer treatment.

- Mix with equal parts of carrot and celery for arthritic conditions.

CARROT JUICE - litre a day. More if desired.

Helps regulate the entire bodily system. Builds healthy tissue - particularly good for the skin and mucus membranes. Consider for ulcers along with cabbage juice and potato juice.

Antiseptic properties benefit throat infections, colds, 'flu and sinus problems.
- Its action on the optic system is well documented. Good for conjunctivitis.

- It helps strengthen the resistance.
- Those of a nervous tendency should take carrot juice daily.

CELERY JUICE - A small wineglass before meals.

- A specific for arthritis, rheumatism and allied conditions.

- Calms an over active nervous system.

POTATO JUICE - A small wineglass twice daily between meals.

- Prescribed for gastritis and stomach troubles, including ulcers.

- Use with carrot and celery juices in equal parts for gout to combat over acidity.

- Potato juice is cleansing in its action.

RADISH JUICE - Diluted, a small sherry glass once or twice daily between meals.

- Stimulates liver, kidney and bladder function.

- Particularly useful for gallstones and gravel.

- Cleansing of catarrhal conditions, especially with horseradish.

- Mix with carrot juice for toning mucous membranes.

TOMATO JUICE - A pint or more daily away from meals.

- Helps neutralise an acid conditioned body.

- Valuable blood purifier. Helps keep the skin clear of acne.

- A good liver decongestant.

- An excellent lactogogue - helps growing babies.

- Combines well with other vegetables.

BIOTTA VEGETABLE JUICE COCKTAIL - As much as desired - any time up to half an hour before meals.

- This specially chosen combination of tomatoes, carrots, celery, and red beetroot is a valuable, easily digestible food which can help neutralise acidity - so should be a regular part of the diet of rheumatics, arthritics, sufferers from gout, liver congestion, gallstones, sinus problems and skin troubles.

BREUSS VEGETABLE JUICE - Two wineglasses a day as a prophylactic supplement to the diet.

- A minimum of a quarter and up to half a litre a day when following the Breuss juice fast.

- Rudolf Breuss maintains his juice, in combination with a healthy diet, will help many distressing complaints. It ensures the body derives the nutrients from live food, an essential part of health and healing.

- Whilst Breuss originally prepared his formula for the dietetic treatment of cancer and leukaemia, it follows that it must have a valuable role wherever there is a depleted vitality - it is nutritious, full of 'life force', so easily assimilated it is a 'natural' for sufferers of other serious diseases like auto-immune deficiency syndrome, M.E., and for nervous exhaustion and those who simply need a dietary tonic to raise their vitality.

- It is indeed a juice par excellence.

There are many more delicious fruit juices and nutritious vegetable juices made in Tagerwilen which are unfortunately not yet available in all countries. For the purposes of this book, I have selected those which are readily available in health food stores, good food shops and some pharmacies in this country.

Readers in Britain requiring further information about the organic juices of Biotta AG should write to their UK agents - Cedar Health Ltd., Pepper Road, Hazel Grove, Stockport, Cheshire SK7 5BW. Readers in other countries should write direct to Biotta AG, Tagerwilen, Switzerland.

Cancer/Leukaemia by Rudolf Breuss is published in English and is available from good health food stores or direct from the UK sole distributors Nuhelth Books, 26 Church Street, Stroud, Glos GL5 1JL.

Hugo Brandenberger with his growing range of Biotta Juices

I N D E X